242413 VA

ICONIC CLASSIC CARS

Kevin Van Campenhout

TABLE OF CONTENTS

PREFACE

This book was born out of frustration – and of a dream. For years I had collected the usual tomes on classic cars, only to be disappointed. Page after page of machines photographed in sterile studios against black backgrounds. Beautiful, yes, but lifeless. These cars were created to move through the world, not to be pinned down like insects under glass. They are myths made real, yet if you are not wealthy enough to wander concours lawns or museum halls, you would be forgiven for wondering if they exist at all.

I wanted something else. The book I could not find. A book that demystifies. That brings the *Mona Lisa*s of the automotive world – the most iconic creations of each marque – back into the light of day. Cars whose histories are as vivid as their forms, presented in colours and settings that reveal their soul. Cars that have graced the lawns of Pebble Beach and Villa d'Este, yes, but also cars unseen in public for decades.

That was the idea. Making it real was something else entirely. From the first shoot to the last, the project took just ten months – ten months to source, secure, and photograph twenty-five of the most important cars ever built. Ten months of short nights, of impossible schedules, of long conversations with owners who had every reason to say no. For most of these machines, the days of being driven outdoors seemed long gone; their rarity, historical significance and sheer financial weight kept them hidden. But slowly, one by one, I convinced their custodians. I showed them the vision. I promised to do these cars justice – not as museum pieces, but as living works of art.

What followed was a journey across time and light. From the 1950s to the early 1980s, I sought to show the evolution of design: from the delicate lines of post-war optimism to the audacious wedges of the supercar era. Diversity was the hardest challenge. Not only in the cars themselves, but in their settings, their colours, their light. Dawn and dusk, sudden rain and the brilliance of the midday sun all became part of the palette. No single hue, no single mood, was allowed to dominate.

And the result? Something close, I hope, to the book of my dreams. Twenty-five stories told in steel, light and shadow. Twenty-five masterpieces reunited not in a museum, but in the world for which they were created. Some had not been seen in the open for decades; their presence here is an exclusive gift, and a reminder of the generosity of the owners who entrusted us with them.

This, then, is not just another book about classic cars. It is an invitation. To stand before the icons of our imagination, and to see them again as they were meant to be: in motion, in light, in life. Some of them, hidden away in private collections, had not felt the open air for decades, and their appearance here is both rare privilege and fleeting miracle.

Kevin Van Campenhout, 2025

GOODYEAR
Agip
27
Marlboro
PIONEER
GOODYEAR
Modena MOTORSPORT
AVON

1950

FERRARI 166 MM BARCHETTA TOURING

LA NONNA

BELGRAVIA, LONDON, GREAT BRITAIN

3

Gianni Agnelli owned many Ferraris, yet the 166 MM held a special place in his memory, as he once recalled: 'Of all the cars I have driven, I can never forget my first Ferrari.'

Tucked into the shadowed hush of a narrow London mews, with weathered brick on either side and wrought-iron gates keeping secrets, the Ferrari 166 MM sits like a whisper from another age. Small, purposeful, impossibly elegant. It doesn't dominate the space – it transforms it. This is the beginning of not just Ferrari's racing legacy, but of modern motor racing itself.

The 166 MM was born for victory. Its full name – *166 Mille Miglia* – was a declaration of purpose, and in 1949, just two years after Enzo Ferrari founded his company, it delivered Ferrari's first major international wins. Behind the wheel of a 166 MM, Clemente Biondetti won the Mille Miglia, while Luigi Chinetti and Lord Selsdon drove it to triumph in the 24 Hours of Le Mans. That same year, another 166 MM also claimed victory at Spa 24 Hours, cementing Ferrari's presence on the international stage.

Light, agile and deceptively fast, it was Ferrari's first true sports racing car – the one that told the world: Maranello had arrived to compete.

Powered by a 2.0-litre Colombo-designed V12 and paired with a five-speed manual gearbox, the car sat on a tubular chassis and weighed under 700 kg. With just 140 horsepower, it could still reach speeds over 210 km/h – blistering for its day. Drum brakes and a live rear axle reflected the era's limits, but its poise and balance made it a serious weapon. It was built to win – and it did.

Only 33 examples of the 166 MM were made, including 25 open spiders by Carrozzeria Touring. Each was subtly different, tailored like a fine Italian suit.

This one, chassis #0064M, belonged first to Gianni Agnelli, the dashing industrialist and future patriarch of Fiat – and later, owner of Ferrari. At 27, Agnelli was already Italy's unofficial prince of style. When he saw the sleek roadster designed by Carrozzeria Touring, he dubbed it what it reminded him of: a little boat. In doing so, he gave the automotive world a new word – *barchetta* – one that would come to define a whole generation of open sports cars made for both road and race.

Delivered on 12 June 1950, chassis #0064M was sold via Milan's Lombardi & Koelliker, having just been completed by Carrozzeria Touring. It wore a unique, elegant livery requested by the future Avvocato: dark blue over deep green, as unorthodox as it was discreet.

At the time, Fiat was still under the watchful control of managing director Vittorio Valletta, and Agnelli was strictly forbidden from driving any car not bearing the family badge. So the Ferrari was acquired in secret. There are no photographs of Agnelli with the car – just a whispered chapter in the early story of a man who would later define Italian automotive culture. After only two years, he sold it. But the legacy of #0064M was just beginning.

166 JCG

The legendary first Ferrari V12 was created by engineer Gioacchino Colombo in 1947 with a displacement of 1.5 litres. It underwent continuous development until 1988.

Carrozzeria Touring, based in Milan, was renowned for its Superleggera construction method. In the 1950s, it was Italy's leading coachbuilder, with many of the earliest Ferraris passing through its workshops.

When Agnelli first laid eyes on it, he christened it 'Barchetta' – an emblematic term was born that very day. The Avvocato, as he was known, also chose the striking blue and green livery for his 166 MM.

Its next chapter unfolded in Belgium, where it was acquired by Vicomte Gery d'Hendecourt. He transformed the car into a full-blooded racer, fitting it with triple Weber 32 DCF carburettors that unleashed its full potential. In 1953, in the hands of a young Olivier Gendebien, who would later become one of Ferrari's most successful endurance drivers, the car won the Coupe de Spa.

Later, another Belgian talent, Jean Blaton – better known by his racing pseudonym 'Beurlys' – added more victories and podiums across local circuits, further enriching the car's growing legend.

In the years that followed, Ferrari dealer and loyalist Jacques Swaters acquired #0064M and gave it a new lease of life. He restored it to its original configuration and preserved it for 46 years. Under his stewardship, the car was more than maintained – it was celebrated. Displayed at MoMA in New York and the Berlin National Gallery, it became a symbol of historic motoring excellence.

Since 2012, its current custodian has carried that legacy forward with dignity. The car has appeared at the Mille Miglia Storica, Pebble Beach, and the Enzo Ferrari Museum in Modena – a quiet return to the spiritual home of the Prancing Horse.

More than just a racing car, the 166 MM is Ferrari's origin story in motion. *La Nonna* (the grandmother) is the spark that lit the fire, on the track and in the imagination. Gianni Agnelli, who would go on to drive many Ferraris, once said that of them all, he would never forget the first – this very car.

That memory, held by Italy's most discerning industrialist, speaks volumes. Just like for Agnelli himself, age has taken away none of its charm. Only the rarest machines manage that trick: to be remembered not just for what they did, but for what they made possible. ■

166
JCG

FERRARI 166 MM BARCHETTA TOURING

1948–1951
25 units produced
V12 engine (1,996 cc)
140 hp
210 km/h

1953

FIAT 8V SUPERSONIC

JET-AGE DREAM

GDYNIA, POLAND

The shape of a space age: in the 1950s, the futurism of jet aircraft set the public imagination alight, and designers drew inspiration from the streamlined forms of reactors.

Chassis #1006*000036 rests quietly on the creaking wooden planks of the Gdynia pier, facing the steel-grey waters of the Baltic Sea. It is bitterly cold, the wind is salted and sharp, and the light dissolves into cloud-like breath into fog. But even here – especially here – this dark red jewel refuses to vanish into the gloom. It gleams. With poise, not noise. With line, not mass. As if someone had left a shooting star parked by the water and it forgot to burn out.

The car is a Fiat, technically. But in truth, it is barely tethered to the world of practical transportation. This is a flight of fantasy – a jet-age reverie carved in metal. And it begins, improbably, with an engine Fiat had no intention of building.

In the early 1950s, Fiat's engineers developed a compact 2.0-litre V8, codenamed '8V' (Otto Vu). They believed – incorrectly – that Ford held a copyright on the name 'V8', and so cleverly flipped the badge to avoid complications. The engine was a marvel for its size: lightweight, high-revving and complex. Yet it had no place in Fiat's mainstream production, which at the time was focused on building cars for an Italy recovering from the Second World War. Nevertheless, the company decided to build a few sporting chassis as a showcase of engineering and as a way to participate discreetly in motorsport. The gamble paid off: the 8V proved remarkably competitive, establishing Fiat as a force in post-war performance motoring.

Only 114 Fiat 8V chassis would ever be made, which is an unusually small batch even for an experimental run. But their mechanical elegance made them a favourite canvas for coachbuilders, and no one painted more vividly than Ghia.

Enter Giovanni Savonuzzi. Savonuzzi had designed a one-off aerodynamic body for a Jaguar XK120 that attempted to break speed records. Though the project failed, the design lived on. Seeing an opportunity to rehouse the shape on a more nimble and compact chassis, Savonuzzi adapted the form for Fiat's new 8V. The result was the 8V Supersonic, a car that had almost nothing in common with Fiat's boxy saloons or even its racing spiders.

Only 14 Fiat 8V chassis would be clothed in this dreamlike Supersonic body by Ghia. And chassis #1006*000036, built in 1953 and finished in a deep, almost wine-like shade of red, is among the most carefully preserved of them all.

Everything about its appearance suggests speed not merely as a number, but as a principle of design. The proportions are exaggerated, but never clumsy: a long bonnet, an impossibly low roofline, and tail fins that taper like the swept wings of a fighter jet. There is

The colourful opulence of a carefree and optimistic era: the dashboard echoes the cherry-red bodywork, as do the piping details of the generous leather upholstery.

The twin C-shaped dials seem borrowed from a science-fiction spacecraft. It doesn't travel at Mach 1, but it comes close to the mythical 200 km/h mark.

a visual velocity to the whole car, even at rest. Chrome strakes glide along its flanks, mimicking air intakes. The windscreen is curved like a pilot's canopy. The headlights sit behind delicate plexiglass fairings. This was not a car made for roads – it was made to look like it could take off.

But the 8V Supersonic was not just a styling exercise. Underneath its aviation skin, the car retained Fiat's advanced mechanical package: the 2.0-litre V8 engine with twin Weber carburettors, capable of pushing out over 110 horsepower, paired to a four-speed manual gearbox. With its light body and rear transaxle, it had near-ideal weight distribution, and though the live rear axle and leaf springs were conventional, the handling was balanced and nimble for the time.

And yet it wasn't about lap times. It was about theatre. The Supersonic's presence was so strong that it became a beacon of post-war optimism, embraced by design tastemakers and industrialists alike. A few Supersonics were built on other chassis – Jaguar XK120s, Aston Martins, even an Alfa Romeo 1900 – but the Fiat versions remained the purest expression of the form. Fiat, the humble everyman brand, had for a brief moment produced a rolling sculpture worthy of a science-fiction film set.

Today, this dark red example with its razor lines, fine details and haunting stance feels almost eerie against the grey void of the Baltic sky. Here, where the sea whispers of cold lands and cold wars, it brings with it an echo of a warmer kind of future: a vision of speed, style and unshakeable confidence. Its elegance is not just speculative – it's proven. After a meticulous restoration, this very car earned Best in Class at the 2017 Concorso d'Eleganza Villa d'Este, reaffirming that Ghia's Supersonic wasn't just a flight of fantasy, but a true classic of concours-winning calibre.

It doesn't shout. It doesn't need to. In an age when cars were machines, this one was a message. And like all good messages from the future, it arrived far too early. ■

Legendary yet short-lived, the Fiat V8 engine – known in Italian as the Otto Vu – was originally conceived to conquer the American market with a large sedan project that never came to fruition.

Aeronautical references are everywhere, from the tapered tail lights to the flowing lines – a style that would cross the Atlantic and become a hallmark of Detroit's automobiles.

FIAT 8V SUPERSONIC

1953
14 units produced
V8 engine (1,996 cc)
110 hp
190 km/h

1954

MASERATI A6GCS/53 PININ FARINA BERLINETTA

THE TRIDENT'S WHISPER

PONT ALEXANDRE III, PARIS, FRANCE

The trident emblem that adorns every Maserati is inspired by the statue of the *Fontana del Nettuno* in Bologna. So could there be a more fitting setting for our photographs than the *Enfant au Poisson* on Paris's Pont Alexandre III?

Dawn over Pont Alexandre III. The city is still wrapped in silence, the Seine barely stirring beneath its gilded arches. Along the bridge's ornate parapet, the genius with a trident leans forward, muscles tensed, weapon drawn, ready to hurl it at some unseen adversary. A symbol of motion frozen in bronze.

Just metres away, another trident glints – smaller, more discreet, but just as loaded with intent. It sits at the tip of a Maserati A6GCS, its sharp lines softened by the pale Parisian light. There's a quiet symmetry to the scene: one trident forged by myth, the other by Modena. Both speak of power, precision and beautifully restrained aggression.

Born in the early 1950s, the A6GCS was Maserati at its purest: a lightweight, front-engined sports car built for privateers to challenge the world's most demanding roads. The name itself tells the story – *A* for Alfieri, the marque's founder; *6* for the number of cylinders; *GCS* for 'Ghisa Corsa Sport', or cast-iron block, racing, sports. This was no grand tourer. It was built for the Mille Miglia, the Targa Florio, for tight corners, rough tarmac and fast hands.

Under its aluminium skin lay a 2.0-litre inline-six, delivering around 170 horsepower, paired with a four-speed manual gearbox and backed by torsion bar front suspension and a live rear axle. That power figure might seem modest by modern standards, but at under 750 kg, the A6GCS moved like mercury – fluid, immediate, alive. Its chassis was predictable at the edge, its balance sublime, its limits high. In the right hands, it was a weapon.

Between 1953 and 1955, it carved a reputation as a giant slayer, with multiple class wins in the Mille Miglia, an overall victory at the 1953 Targa Florio in the hands of Sergio Mantovani, and strong showings at Monza, Pescara and Imola.

But where it truly defied expectation was in its form. The story goes that heavy rains during the 1952 Mille Miglia left drivers of the open A6GCS exposed and exhausted, prompting customers to ask Maserati for a closed version of the car. The task was entrusted to Pinin Farina (renamed 'Pininfarina' from the sixties onwards), whose hand gave the coupé a purity rarely seen in racing machinery. The long, fluid fenders, the taut roofline, the barely-there tail – every line served a purpose, yet the result was poetry. Only a handful were ever built. Some raced. Some crashed. A few survived. But each one carries within it a piece of Maserati's soul before the brand turned its focus to road-going GTs.

What you see here is much more than a car. It is a reunion – a marriage of two parallel histories, stitched together across decades, borders and racing eras.

The story begins with chassis #2057, one of only four A6GCS Berlinettas ever bodied by Pinin Farina. Delivered in January 1954, it made its public debut

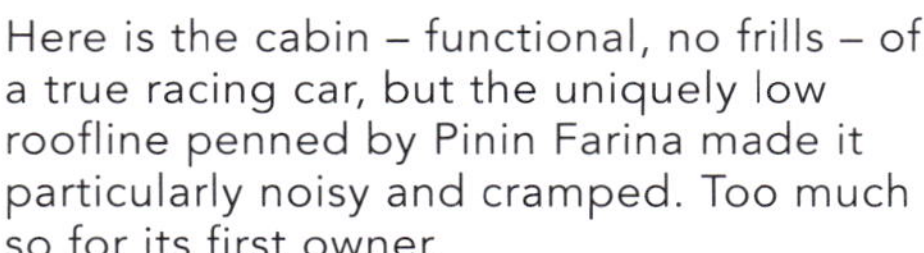
Here is the cabin – functional, no frills – of a true racing car, but the uniquely low roofline penned by Pinin Farina made it particularly noisy and cramped. Too much so for its first owner.

The cars were commissioned through the Rome dealer Guglielmo Dei - Maserati could reach Pinin Farina only by this discreet path, as the coachbuilder was bound by contract to Ferrari.

Six cylinders, three twin-choke carburettors, yet no fewer than twelve spark plug leads: the cast-iron engine block of the Maserati A6GCS was innovative for its time, featuring a pioneering twin-ignition system.

at the Turin Motor Show that spring, dazzling crowds in a daring two-tone blue, with a red leather interior as theatrical as it was luxurious. Its first owner, Pietro Palmieri of Rome, was a gentleman racer: light in stature, he asked Pinin Farina to give his Berlinetta a lower roofline, sculpted to fit him – and only him.

But that unique detail would seal its fate. After entering the 1954 Giro dell'Umbria, where it finished 7th under the punishing summer sun, Palmieri soured on the experience. The cabin was simply too cramped, too hot, too loud. In frustration, he had the coachwork removed and replaced with a barchetta body. The original Pinin Farina shell, that rolling sculpture, was quietly set aside.

And so enters chassis #2070, a Spyder bodied by Fiandri & Malagoli, built in April 1954 for Dr Vialiano Peduzzi before passing into the hands of French rider Georges Monneret. He campaigned it hard, with podiums across France and a notable win in the 1954 Coupe d'Automne at Montlhéry. Later sold to Jean Thépenier, Maserati's importer in France, the car was eventually dismantled.

Years later, both relics – #2057's Pinin Farina coupe body and #2070's bare chassis – found their way into the collection of Marc Nicolosi, the man behind Paris's Rétromobile. But it wasn't until 1997 that a new owner dared to complete the story: reuniting the original Berlinetta body with a proper A6GCS soul. A machine built twice, but never compromised. A sculpture that waited half a century to become whole again.

To see it here in Paris, parked beneath the trident of the genius, is to feel the pull of two worlds – myth and machinery, sculpture and speed. The bridge beneath the wheels is ornate, baroque, gilded. The car above it is raw, pure, elemental. Together, they create something timeless. A fleeting harmony between elegance and force. ■

MASERATI A6GCS/53 PININ FARINA BERLINETTA

1953–1954
4 units produced
Straight-six engine (1,985.5 cc)
170 hp
235 km/h

JAGUAR D-TYPE

DESIGNED TO DOMINATE

FLEMISH COUNTRYSIDE, BELGIUM

49

A car defined by its unique bodywork: the Jaguar D-Type is instantly recognisable by the distinctive vertical fin rising behind the driver – an aerodynamic appendage designed to improve stability at high speed on the straights.

There's a particular kind of silence to the Flemish countryside. The kind that hangs between red-brick barns and weather-worn shutters, where time gathers like dust on cobblestones. Into this stillness rolls a shape that feels both alien and perfectly placed: the Jaguar D-Type, deep green and impossibly low, crouched like a big cat at rest.

It feels like the air around it remembers something. A hum of past violence. A ripple of speed. Because this was not built for stillness. This was built for Le Mans.

Unveiled in 1954, the D-Type wasn't just a successor to Jaguar's C-Type, but a radical rethinking of what a racing car could be. Where others built cars, Jaguar engineered a machine. Its monocoque chassis, derived from aircraft construction, was revolutionary: stronger, lighter and sturdier than anything on the grid. Over it, designer Malcolm Sayer sculpted a body with aerodynamic efficiency that still stops hearts 70 years later.

Under the long bonnet lay the legendary 3.4-litre straight-six XK engine, fed by triple Weber carburettors and capable of pushing the D-Type to over 260 km/h – staggering figures for the era. The car's fin, rising like a dorsal blade behind the driver's headrest, wasn't just theatrical – it provided genuine high-speed stability on the Mulsanne Straight.

And it worked. Le Mans, 1955: 1st place. Le Mans, 1956: again. And then, in 1957, a near-mythical sweep: five of the top six places were taken by D-Types, including the top three. It was the kind of dominance that changes the sport. That final year, however, marked Jaguar's official exit from factory racing. The D-Type's reign had been short, but it was absolute.

Of the 71 Jaguar D-Types built between 1954 and 1956, 53 were destined for privateer teams, and among them was chassis #XKD 523, a car that retained the short, steeply raked nose of the early works racers. This snub-nosed design, more compact and aggressive, would soon give way to the long-nose variant developed for Jaguar's factory entries at Le Mans, engineered to carve through the high-speed straights with greater aerodynamic efficiency. But the early cars – like this one – remain the purest expression of the D-Type's original design intent: raw, focused and unmistakably fast.

#XKD 523 left Coventry on 22 November 1955, painted black over red, and was shipped across the Atlantic to Roberts Harrison, who quickly sold it to Walter Huggler. It was Huggler who first unleashed the car on the track, taking victory at Allentown in

49

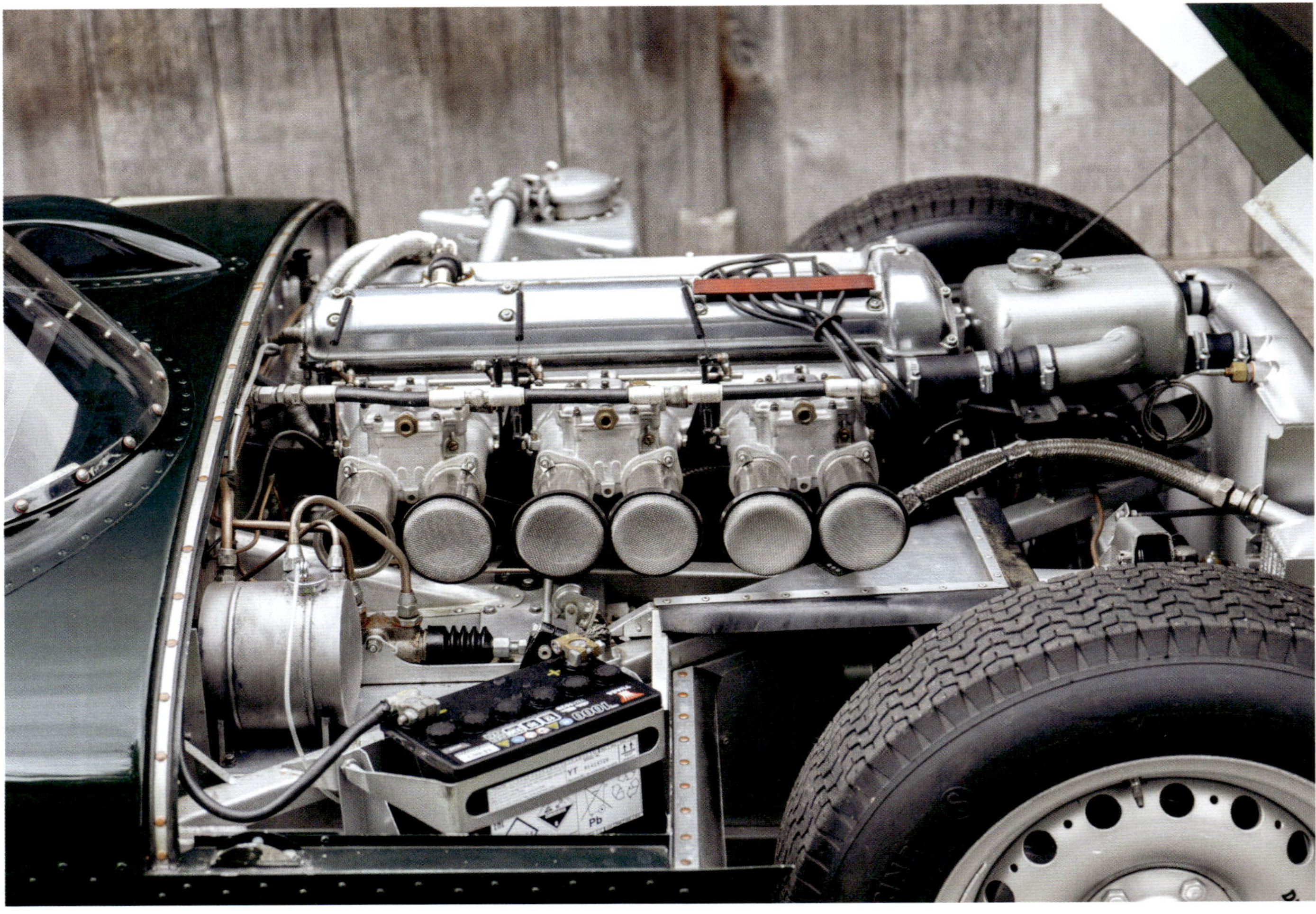

An engine that became part of legend: Jaguar's inline-six 'XK' was the first to propel a road car past the 200 km/h mark, when it debuted in the Jaguar XK120.

Between 1951 and 1957, Jaguar won the 24 Hours of Le Mans five times. In the 1950s, the brand was at its peak – a true sporting rival to Ferrari. But the story was brief: nothing would surpass the legacy of the D-Type.

The sporting regulations of the 24 Hours of Le Mans required cars to have two seats, but nothing prevented teams from covering the passenger-side opening to gain an aerodynamic advantage.

August 1956. That season, the D-Type also appeared at Watkins Glen and competed in the Governor's Trophy at Nassau, the Caribbean crown jewel of the racing calendar, where it finished a respectable 12th among a grid of elite machinery and star drivers.

Its next chapter took a turn that was no less dramatic. The car was acquired by drag racer Joe Grimaldi, who blew the engine during a record attempt at Daytona Beach. Undeterred, he fitted a Buick V8 into the Jaguar's chassis, heavily modifying the car in the process – an act of mechanical audacity, if not preservation.

In 1965, Jeff Millstein took ownership and began the slow and careful process of returning the D-Type to its original configuration. A new front subframe was installed, while the original components were shipped to England, where Lister – famed for its Jaguar-based racers – used them to construct a replica.

But the true resurrection would come decades later. The car's current guardian, determined to reunite the fragmented legacy, tracked down that Lister replica and reacquired the subframe that once belonged to #XKD 523. In 2008, those original parts were finally returned to their rightful place.

Today, in a farm courtyard west of Brussels, there's no roar – only the creak of timber and the soft sigh of wind. And yet the D-Type remains electric. Every line is taut with purpose, from the sculpted nose to the raised fin. Its cockpit – offset, spartan and wrapped in riveted alloy – still smells faintly of oil, leather and ghosts.

Here, where ploughs once rested, now sits a racing legend. The barn doors might be closed, but make no mistake: this car still watches for the flag to drop. ■

49

JAGUAR D-TYPE

1954–1957
71 units produced
Straight-six engine (3,442 cc on the earliest cars)
250 hp
260 km/h

1955

MERCEDES-BENZ 300 SL 'GULLWING'

WINGS OF STARDOM

DUBAI DESERT, UNITED ARAB EMIRATES

237421 ROMA

The gullwing doors of the 300 SL gave it an iconic silhouette. This wasn't mere aesthetic flair – it was a direct consequence of the car's chassis architecture.

As the first light spills across the desert and the sky shifts from indigo to soft gold, a figure emerges on the horizon – low, sculpted, unmistakable. The Mercedes-Benz 300 SL Coupé – or 'Gullwing' – doesn't just arrive. It *lands*. Here, against the stillness of the Arabian sands, the car's shimmering bodywork seems to trap the first light of day, while its signature doors reach for the sky like wings ready to take off. It looks otherworldly. Because it is.

Born from the brutal glory of post-war endurance racing, the Mercedes-Benz 300 SL was never intended to be ordinary. Its origins lie in the company's triumphant return to motorsport in 1952, just seven years after the end of the war. The car that laid the foundation – the W194 racing prototype – stunned the world by winning that year's 24 Hours of Le Mans, taking 1st and 2nd, and then conquering the unforgiving Carrera Panamericana in Mexico with a victory that sealed its legend. It was fast, efficient and, above all, resilient – racing over thousands of kilometres across rugged terrain without breaking stride.

The secret lay in the ultralight tubular spaceframe chassis, a radical design that gave the car its strength and agility, but left no room for conventional doors. The solution? A dramatic set of top-hinged gullwing doors – a technical necessity that became a visual signature. When Mercedes decided to bring the car to the road, this innovation was retained, and instantly made the 300 SL Gullwing one of the most recognisable silhouettes ever created in automotive design.

Under the bonnet was another revolution. The 300 SL became the first production car in the world to feature direct fuel injection, developed from aviation technology and adapted for the road. Its 3.0-litre straight-six engine, producing 215 horsepower, propelled the car to a then-staggering top speed of 228 km/h – faster than any other production vehicle of the era. It was a racing car made civil, yet never truly tamed. The perfect marriage of German engineering at its most ambitious and a cinematic sense of drama.

And cinema, as it turned out, loved the Gullwing. Sophia Loren, the queen of 1950s and '60s Italian cinema, famously owned one, and it arrived like a scene from a film. A gift from her husband, producer

237421•ROMA

ROMA 23
7421

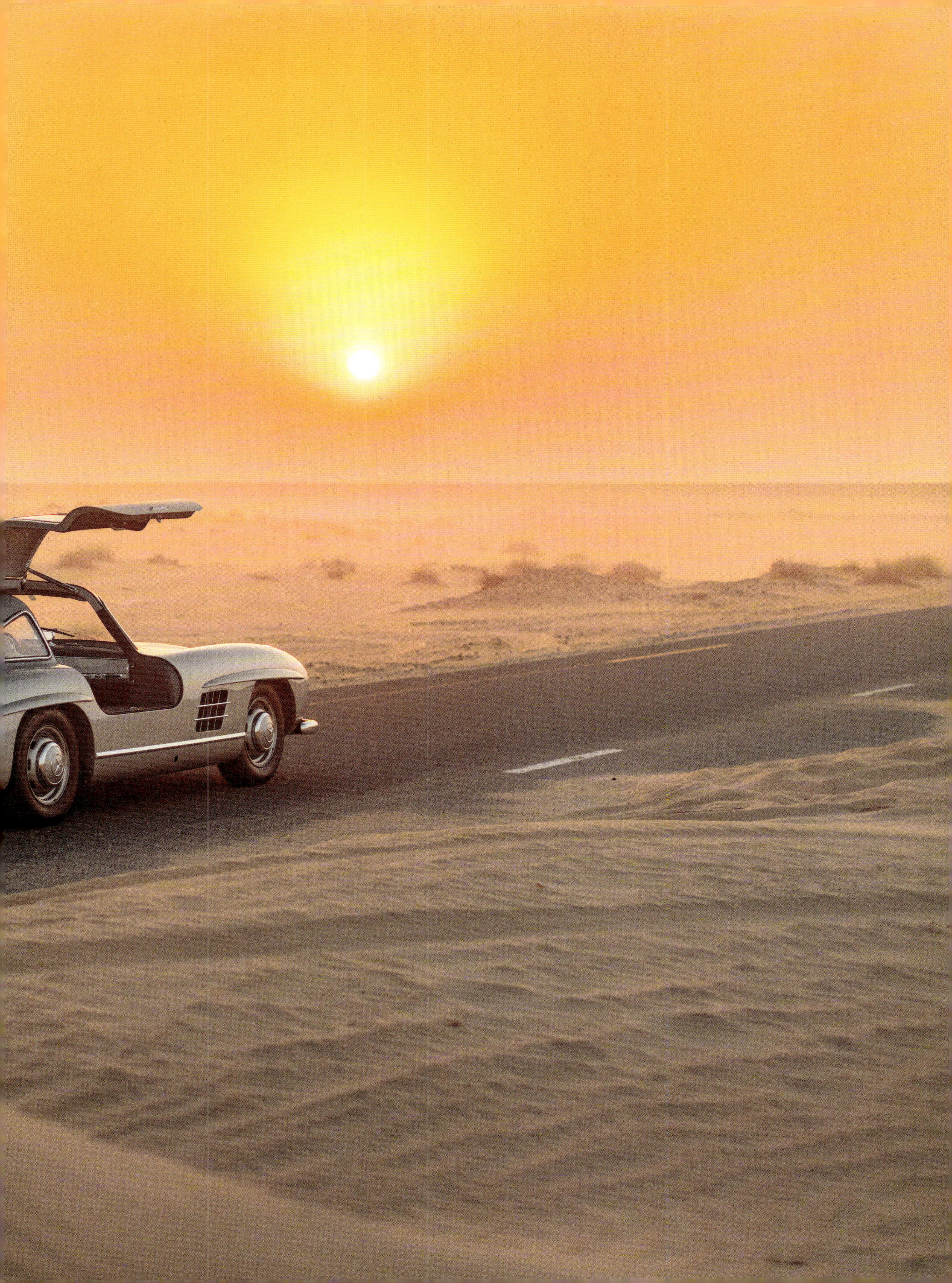

237421 ROMA

Climbing in seems impossible at first, but there's a clever trick: the steering wheel is articulated, tilting downwards to free up legroom and make entry possible.

Technically, it was the most advanced car of its era, yet the baroque aesthetic details were designed to charm an American clientele hungry for chrome.

Carlo Ponti, the Mercedes-Benz 300 SL appeared one morning of October 1955 in the garden of Sophia Loren's Roman villa, its famous doors lifted skywards. The car was finished in the metallic shade made famous by the Silver Arrows of Grand Prix glory, with a blue leather interior. This was chassis #198.040.5500789, and it wore the registration *237421 ROMA*, a plate that still adorns the car today.

Loren, then at the height of her *La Dolce Vita* stardom, took to the Gullwing with affection and flair. The car appeared beside her in a number of captivating period photographs, but the most memorable outing may have been her participation in the III Rally del Cinema, held on 13 April 1956 – a regularity race for Italy's film and television elite. The route ran from Rome to Sanremo, winding through the hills of Siena. It was a whimsical event, ultimately won by the actor Alberto Sordi in his Alfa Romeo Giulietta.

Like many love affairs in cinema, this one was brief. By 10 December 1956, Loren had sold the car to a Roman businessman, moving on, as stars often do, to the next chapter. The Gullwing, however, continued its journey. It passed through the hands of several Italian owners before making its way to the United States, and, eventually, back to Europe.

In 2019, the car was fully restored by German marque specialist HK-Engineering and returned to the precise specifications of its Roman heyday. Today, under the golden light of the Persian Gulf, the car once again lives a life of elegance: polished, poised and protected.

Even today, in a world saturated with supercars and luxury badges, the Gullwing remains instantly recognisable. It is the car that everyone knows – even those who know nothing about cars. A silhouette etched into memory. A design so timeless, it feels like it was carved out of the future.

It may have started as a machine built to win races. But somewhere along the way, it became something else entirely. A symbol. A sculpture. A star. ■

MERCEDES-BENZ 300 SL 'GULLWING'

1954–1957
1,400 units produced
Straight-six engine (2,996 cc)
215 hp
228 km/h

PORSCHE 550 SPYDER

ICE IN ITS VEINS

ZELL AM SEE, AUSTRIA

ZE LL 550

Not just a charming postcard: the Austrian mountains around Zell am See witnessed the birth of Porsche's sports car adventure.

On a clear winter morning, the ice lies frozen in silence, its glassy surface unbroken but for a single machine. Low, white and sinewed like a clenched muscle, the Porsche 550 Spyder sits motionless, its poised stillness promising violence at speed. You'd almost think it was born here. And in a way, it was.

Zell am See, cradled by the Austrian Alps, is not just a backdrop. It is ancestral ground – a place where the Porsche family found both refuge and purpose. In the early post-war years, Ferdinand Porsche retired here, and the family would return again and again. Here, among these peaks, they didn't just build cars. They tested them – on snow, on ice, on circuits carved into the winter.

The ice races on Lake Zell became the stuff of legend. From 1937 to 1974, this frozen expanse was a gleaming battlefield where engines roared, tyres clawed for grip, and spectators – skiers and townsfolk alike – lined the snowy banks and cheered as drivers slid through corners at full tilt. It was more than a race. It was theatre on ice. And at the centre of the drama, always: Porsche.

In 1952, the event took on a deeper meaning. Renamed the Professor Ferdinand Porsche Memorial Race, it became a tribute to the brand's founder, who had passed away the year before. What had started as an alpine curiosity transformed into a celebration – not only of speed, but of legacy. And what better symbol of that era than the 550 Spyder?

Launched in 1953, the 550 was Porsche's first true racing car: a clean-sheet design, born not from a road car, but for victory. Light, flat and perfectly balanced, it carried the 1.5-litre four-cam Fuhrmann engine, mounted low in a tubular frame. It was a weapon in the hands of masters: Hans Herrmann, Umberto Maglioli, Richard von Frankenberg. It won at Carrera Panamericana, Targa Florio and its class at Le Mans, bringing Porsche international acclaim and its first taste of legend.

But there were two sides to the 550. After the factory built its initial racing run, Porsche answered demand from wealthy privateers and gentleman racers with a second series: the customer Spyders. These cars shared the same bones – lightweight, brutally efficient – but were trimmed with just a hint more civility. Slightly raised windscreens, hand-finished touches, perhaps even a passenger seat. Not road cars exactly, but racing cars that could be lived with. Barely.

The car pictured here, #550-0018, tells the beginning of this chapter of the 550 Spyder story. Assembled in January 1955, it was one of the first three customer cars, all painted white at the factory and adorned with flames across the rear – red, in this case. Though it doesn't wear the lowest chassis number of the second series (which began with #0016), it was in fact the first built – a prototype of sorts for Porsche's new generation of customer racers.

ZE LL 550

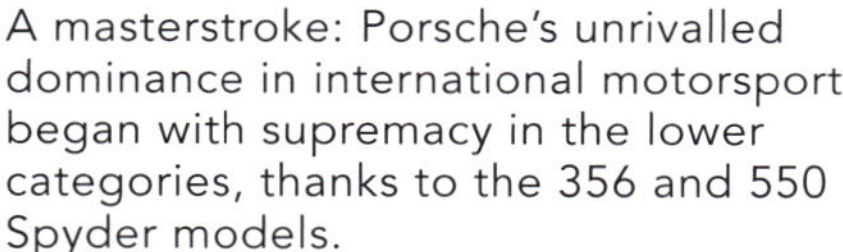
A masterstroke: Porsche's unrivalled dominance in international motorsport began with supremacy in the lower categories, thanks to the 356 and 550 Spyder models.

Beneath the rear bonnet of the 550 sat the Fuhrmann Type 547 engine, an evolution of the 356's air-cooled flat-four, now with four overhead camshafts.

Subtlety in the details: beneath the slender framework, a single exhaust pipe rises proudly.

Studded tyres, ready to bite into the ice of the very same frozen circuit where it made its debut 70 years ago.

It was personally used by Ferry Porsche and later entered by Huschke von Hanstein, Porsche's Competition Director, in the Lake Zell ice race, where it first met the frozen surface it would one day return to.

Shortly after, it was delivered to its first official owner, Kurt Ahrens, a talented German privateer and father of the future Porsche factory ace Kurt Ahrens Jr. Racing across Europe, Ahrens scored numerous good results in the car, including a win at the 1955 Grand Prix of Bordeaux. In 1956, it passed to Sepp Liebl, who campaigned it in the gruelling 1,000 km of the Nürburgring, finishing top of its class.

Though later restored in silver, #550-0018 has recently been returned to its original livery – white with red flames, beige upholstery, and the charming early details of the very first customer cars: no air inlets on the nose, just a subtle chrome trim with a rubber seal.

And in a moment of poetic symmetry, the car returned in 2019 to the same ice where it first made tracks. Reborn as the F.A.T. Ice Race, the legendary event was revived by Ferdinand Porsche, great-grandson of the marque's founder and namesake of the memorial race. Once again, #550-0018 glided across the frozen Lake Zell, linking Porsche's past to its living tradition.

In the very same place that once echoed with the sound of studded tyres and flat-fours at redline, today, the 550 returns. Silent, but never still. A ghost of speed. A glint of red in a world of white. And still, unmistakably alive. ■

ZE LL 550

PORSCHE 550 SPYDER

1953–1956
90 units produced
Flat-four engine (1,498 cc)
110 hp
220 km/h

1958

BMW 507

ALPINE GRACE, HOLLYWOOD HEAT

CANTON OF BERN, SWITZERLAND

There's no coincidence here: the white BMW makes its way through the Canton of Bern in Switzerland, the birthplace of actress Ursula Andress, its most famous owner. A gift from Elvis Presley – what a story!

There are cars that speak of engineering. And then there are cars that sing of desire. The BMW 507 does both – softly, powerfully, like a jazz ballad gliding through the curves of the Alps.

Photographed here amidst the quiet charm of the Bernese countryside, the 507 looks almost too perfect, like a visiting movie star who somehow belongs. This isn't just a machine parked in a postcard. It's an echo of a time when elegance came with a straight-six growl and style was measured in chrome and leather.

Designed by Albrecht von Goertz, the 507 was BMW's answer to the American roadster boom – but it was no mere competitor. It was a statement. Low-slung and impossibly graceful, it spoke to a more refined kind of speed. One that didn't need to shout.

The BMW 507 is much more than a pretty face. Beneath its flowing lines beats a 3.2-litre V8 engine, producing around 150 horsepower – a remarkable figure for the mid-1950s. Thanks to its lightweight aluminium engine block and a tubular steel frame, the car weighs just over 1,100 kg, enabling a quick, nimble drive with zero to 60 mph achieved in just over eight seconds.

Its suspension system was equally advanced for its time: independent front double wishbones paired with a live rear axle struck a delicate balance between sporty handling and everyday comfort. The interior combined craftsmanship with elegance, featuring a wood-rimmed steering wheel, leather upholstery and tasteful chrome detailing.

Though the 507 never reached mass production numbers – only 252 were made – it was BMW's bold statement of technical innovation and style. Each car was handcrafted with care, embodying a rare blend of performance and sophistication.

Elvis knew beauty when he saw it. Stationed in Germany, the King of Rock and Roll fell under the spell of the BMW 507 – a machine of such elegance, it made even Cadillacs seem clumsy. He bought one for himself. Years later, when love – or something like it – brought him to the Swiss-born actress Ursula Andress, he offered her a Cadillac convertible. She declined. She wanted a BMW too.

Thus, the white 507 with red leather interior – chassis #70192, completed on 30 November 1958 – found its way to Ursula, then living under the golden light of the California sun. For nearly fifteen years,

BE·2618·U

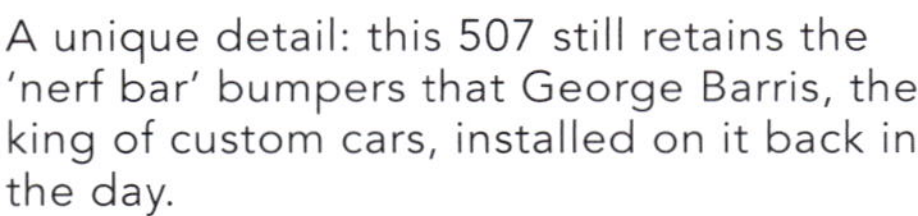

A unique detail: this 507 still retains the 'nerf bar' bumpers that George Barris, the king of custom cars, installed on it back in the day.

BMW's very first V8 was designed for the luxury 502 sedan, and the company would not produce another V8 for the next 30 years.

Ursula Andress wanted the same BMW as Elvis Presley – and that's how the King gifted her a white 507, just like his own.

it was more than just her car. It was her constant companion, her slice of Bavarian elegance on the Pacific coast.

But California had its own ideas about style. The car was serviced by none other than George Barris, the crowned prince of American custom culture. And Barris, never one to leave well enough alone, did what many would call unthinkable: he replaced the original German engine with a Ford 289 V8, swapped in a new transmission, lowered the stance and added a pair of flamboyant nerf bar bumpers. The 507, in its Hollywood phase, became louder, lower, brasher. In short: it became Ursula, the actress whose role as the first ever James Bond girl made her into a superstar.

Time passed. The car changed hands again. But its next custodian saw past the chrome and kitsch, back to the purity of the machine beneath. A proper BMW V8 and gearbox were sourced. Piece by piece, the 507 was brought back to life as it had first existed, save for one detail. The Barris bumpers, too brazen to ignore, too much a part of the car's strange and glamorous journey, remain. A memory in metal. A whisper of scandal.

And yet, here it is, returned not just to Europe, but to Bern. The land of timbered farmhouses, slate roofs and alpine quiet. The place where Ursula Andress herself was born, long before Malibu's sun kissed her skin or Hollywood cast her in gold.

BMW never built another car quite like it. The losses were too great, the ambition too uncompromising. But in that failure lies a kind of poetry. The 507 wasn't meant to be practical – it was too perfect for that. It was a roadster shaped by ideals, not spreadsheets. And now, here in the quiet of the Bernese countryside, it feels not like a return, but a resolution. A sculpture in motion, home at last. ■

BE·2618·U

BMW 507

1956–1959
252 units produced
V8 engine (3,168 cc on the earliest cars)
150 hp
195 km/h

1960

FERRARI 250 GT SWB BERLINETTA COMPETIZIONE

GOD SAVE THE QUEEN

CITY OF WESTMINSTER, LONDON, GREAT BRITAIN

1
60 SWB

With a shortened wheelbase, the Ferrari 250 GT continued its dominance in motorsport, and its more compact, muscular proportions make it, for many, one of the most beautiful Ferraris ever created.

It is said that monarchy isn't just a matter of lineage – it's also about bearing. And if any machine ever carried itself like it belonged among kings, it was this: the Ferrari 250 GT SWB. Low, lean and imperious, it looks entirely at ease on Pall Mall, the ceremonial spine of Westminster where history and royalty meet. Gilded crests hang above old stone façades, and the 250's golden bodywork – subtle, not showy – glows like regalia beneath the grey London sky.

Introduced in 1959, the 250 GT SWB (for 'short wheelbase', or *passo corto*, as they say in Italy) was a response to both engineering necessity and racing ambition. With a wheelbase reduced to 2,400 mm, it was over 200 mm shorter than its predecessor, the 250 GT LWB. The result was sharper handling, faster transitions, and a chassis that responded like a living thing. Wrapped in thin, hand-beaten Scaglietti alloy bodywork, it was also light at just over 950 kg in Competizione trim. The combination was electric: quicker acceleration, better cornering, and far greater composure at the limit.

At its heart was the latest evolution of Gioacchino Colombo's legendary 3.0-litre V12 – an engine that had powered every great Ferrari since the brand's birth. In the SWB, it was tuned to perfection: 280 horsepower at 7,000 rpm for racing versions, and just under 240 hp for the street cars. With Weber 36 DCL3 carburettors, a dry sump in Competizione cars and four-wheel disc brakes (a first for Ferrari GTs), the 250 SWB was among the most technically advanced GT cars of its time.

But statistics don't tell the whole story. The 250 SWB won because it was *balanced*. It had the rare ability to make even an average driver feel like a champion, and in the hands of greats like Stirling Moss, Wolfgang von Trips and Willy Mairesse, it was nearly untouchable. From the Tour de France Automobile (won three times consecutively) to Goodwood, Spa, Le Mans and Sebring, the SWB built Ferrari's reputation for dominance in GT racing.

This is one of those machines whose presence feels earned, not inherited – chassis #2159GT, completed on 28 September 1960, the 44th Ferrari 250 GT SWB to leave Maranello. Clad in the rare and regal hue of *Oro Metallizzato*, with a defiant red nose like war paint, it was never built to hide.

Delivered to Gérard Spinedi, a gentleman racer from Geneva, it was immediately pressed into combat. The car bore was specially modified for that life: twin spotlights in the grille, a chase light mounted on the bonnet for his co-driver to trigger, and even a third windscreen wiper, arcing from the roofline – every inch a tool of function over form.

In March 1961, the gold Ferrari faced the brutal Lyon–Charbonnières–Stuttgart–Solitude Rally, battling

60
SWB

Rallye LYON-
CHARBONNIERES
STUTTGART-SOLITUDE
1
60 SWB

Painted in *Oro Metallizzato* with a hint of red above its grille, this 250 GT SWB Competizione proudly wears the colours it bore during the gruelling 1961 Lyon–Charbonnières–Stuttgart–Solitude Rally.

The pivoting chase light on the left front fender was at the co-driver's disposal to illuminate, for instance, a road sign during gruelling rally stages.

Inside, the cabin – welcoming with its broad leather trim and plush carpets – reminds you that this 250 GT was born a racing car, with its minimalist dashboard and purpose-driven layout.

The most legendary Ferrari engine: the 3.0-litre Colombo V12, delivering 250 cc per cylinder – a figure that would give its name to the entire line of cars equipped with it.

Another unique feature of chassis #2159GT: a third windscreen wiper, mounted at the top of the glass in front of the driver, ensuring optimal visibility during special stages.

across alpine roads shrouded in snow. Paired with a young and daring Jo Schlesser, later to race in Formula 1, they were forced to retire mid-rally, but not before Schlesser drove it to victory on the Solitude circuit stage in Germany.

The Spinedi saga didn't end there. Gérard's navigator in many of these battles was his wife, Aghdass, and together they took the SWB to numerous class wins and podiums in regional rallies. But the real prize was the Tour de France Automobile – a leviathan of endurance and precision. They retired in 1961 and 1962, but in 1963, they returned to finish 4th overall, clinching 3rd in their class, a triumph that etched their names into Ferrari folklore.

In the years since, #2159GT has lived many lives. It has roared back through the historic Tour Auto not once but four times, stretched its legs at Goodwood, and sat quiet, gleaming, under the spotlight at Pebble Beach and Villa d'Este.

There's something ironic about parking a machine born for the heat of the racetrack on royal ground. But then again, Ferrari's greatest creations have always understood duality. The SWB was both athlete and aristocrat. Brutal and beautiful. It's why so many consider it the ultimate GT – the one that got it just right.

And chassis #2159GT embodies that balance to perfection. Worn by competition, shaped by purpose, it carries the quiet authority of something that has earned its elegance. The scars have faded, but the spirit remains, undiluted by time or polish.

Now it rests here, along the route where queens are crowned and emperors once paraded. And yet, it looks neither out of place nor nostalgic. It looks eternal. ■

1

FERRARI 250 GT SWB BERLINETTA COMPETIZIONE

1959–1962
70 units produced
V12 engine (2,953 cc)
270–290 hp
250 km/h

1962

ASTON MARTIN DB4 GT ZAGATO

THE LAST OF THE LINE

GREATER MANCHESTER, GREAT BRITAIN

BUFFET
&
SUNDAY
CARVERY
BOOK EXCHANGE
37PH

BOOK EXCHANGE
BOOK EXCHANGE
37PH

This is not a colourised postcard from 1962: some corners of the English countryside have remained unchanged for six decades. The perfect setting to immortalise this classic Aston Martin in its unique hue.

It stands at ease, angled just so between the neat red phone box and the timeworn brick of a northern English house. The *Caribbean Blue* paintwork looks almost wet under the dull light, as though it has been freshly drawn from a painter's palette. There is no dramatic gesture here, no cinematic fog or racetrack backdrop – just a quiet street in a quiet town near Manchester. And yet, even here, the DB4 GT Zagato has a presence that seems to bend the ordinary around it. It turns stillness into tension, nostalgia into reverence.

This is chassis #0189/R, the very last Aston Martin DB4 GT Zagato ever built. The DB4 GT Zagato story is one of quiet obsession and uncompromising taste. In the late 1950s, Aston Martin was battling the likes of Ferrari and Maserati on both the road and the track. The standard DB4 had already impressed the world, but the DB4 GT – a shortened, lightened and more powerful version – was something altogether sharper. And yet, in Newport Pagnell's eyes, it wasn't quite enough.

Aston turned to Italy, to Zagato, the Milanese coachbuilder known for its featherlight aluminium bodies and keen sense of drama. Ercole Spada, a young designer at Zagato, was tasked with translating the DB4 GT's athleticism into something even more elemental. His creation – lower, slimmer, purer – was both sensual and aggressive, more Latin than English in its contours. The lines were taut but curving, like a thoroughbred coiled mid-stride.

Underneath the sculpted aluminium skin beat Aston's legendary Tadek Marek-designed inline-six, here tuned to 3.7 litres and equipped with twin spark plugs and triple Weber 45 DCOE carburettors. It produced over 310 horsepower – extraordinary for its day – and was paired with a close-ratio four-speed gearbox. Lightweight Perspex windows and pared-down trim made it nearly 100 kg lighter than the DB4 GT. Zero to 60 mph came in just over six seconds; top speed was around 245 km/h. By early 1960s standards, this was a missile.

But it was a missile with manners. The DB4 GT Zagato had poise on the road and promise on the racetrack. And yet, it was built at exactly the wrong moment. Ferrari's 250 GTO was coming, as were the mid-engined revolutionaries from Lotus and Cooper. The Zagato's blend of front-engine balance and hand-formed beauty suddenly felt older than it was.

Aston Martin had originally planned to build 25 examples. In the end, just 19 were completed between 1960 and 1962, making it one of the rarest and most sought-after post-war GTs. And #0189/R, built in 1962, was the very last of them. It is also the only one painted *Caribbean Blue* from the factory.

Everywhere, leather; exquisite bucket seats; yet a simple dashboard in black vermiculated metal: this is the atmosphere of the first Aston Martin GTs designed for racing.

Most DB4 GT Zagatos were delivered in traditional Aston hues of green, silver or racing red. But this final car was destined for something else. Ordered new by Mr S Miller of Horsham, a private client in the UK, it was finished with a delicate, slightly metallic blue over a contrasting red interior. It is, perhaps, the most elegant shade ever laid on such a purposeful shape.

In 1967, the car passed into the hands of Ken Hobbs, who entered it in the Aston Martin Owners Club hill climb at Wiscombe. To improve grip, he subtly flared the rear arches to accommodate wider tyres – a nod to its underlying performance potential. In 1970, the Zagato embarked on a new chapter, this time on South African soil. Over the following decades, it changed hands and colours more than once, before eventually returning to its homeland. In 1995, Aston Martin Works undertook a meticulous restoration, returning the car to its original *Caribbean Blue* and reinstating its first registration: 37PH.

Now, here it is, back in the land where it was born, photographed against the kind of ordinary British backdrop that once shaped the lives of those who built it. The red phone box, the worn flagstones, the scent of old bricks after rain: there's something fitting about this setting.

In chassis #0189/R, the story ends with a flourish of grace. The last of its kind, but also perhaps the most refined. A car that didn't need to prove itself with lap times or headlines. It needed only to exist, quietly, beautifully and completely. Even now, six decades on, it does just that. ■

Aluminium block and head, dual overhead camshafts and twin ignition: the straight-six Aston Martin engine designed by Tadek Marek is a legend in its own right.

ASTON MARTIN DB4 GT ZAGATO

1960–1962
19 units produced
Straight-six engine (3,670 cc)
310 hp
245 km/h

1962

FERRARI 250 GTO

THE GIOCONDA OF FERRARIS

VILLA D'ESTE, LAKE COMO, ITALY

86

8·6

One of the most iconic and successful racing GTs in history. Its three characteristic D-shaped intakes optimise cooling, while three more, invisible, lie beneath the nose.

Some cars define an era. The Ferrari 250 GTO transcends it. More than a masterpiece, it is for some the most iconic car ever built, the crown jewel of automotive history. Revered for its performance, its rarity and, above all, its presence, the GTO is often called the 'Gioconda of Ferraris'. Like Da Vinci's masterpiece, it isn't just admired – it's studied. An object of fascination, mystique and near-mythical status.

Framed by the timeless splendour of Villa d'Este, the GTO is not a guest, but a peer. Built in the 16th century as a cardinal's lakeside retreat, the villa has hosted emperors, artists and royalty for over 500 years. Today, it is also home to the Concorso d'Eleganza Villa d'Este, one of the world's most exclusive showcases of automotive beauty and heritage. Its terraced gardens, carved stone and baroque poise are a fitting match for a car that represents the very summit of Italian craftsmanship. This is not just a backdrop. It is a dialogue between two facets of Italian genius: one born of art and elegance, the other forged in aluminium and fire.

Every curve of the GTO is a declaration. From its flowing fenders to its purposeful stance, it is equal parts racing car and sculpture – form following function with poetic precision. Like the *Mona Lisa*'s smile, its lines are open to interpretation: subtle, sensual and perpetually mysterious. Is it a racing machine? A design sculpture? A national treasure? The answer, of course, is always yes.

Beneath the Ferrari 250 GTO's sculpted body lies the DNA of a thoroughbred. Built between 1962 and 1964, only 36 examples were ever produced. It was Ferrari's final front-engined GT car especially built for top-level racing, and perhaps its most celebrated creation.

At its heart beats a 3.0-litre Colombo V12, an engine as sonorous as it is sophisticated. With six twin-choke Weber carburettors feeding 300 horsepower through a five-speed manual gearbox, the GTO was built not only to race, but to dominate. And it did exactly that, winning the FIA's International Championship for GT Manufacturers in '62, '63 and '64 as well as countless individual victories.

But what made the GTO transcendent wasn't just speed. It was *balance*. Handling tuned by engineer Giotto Bizzarrini before his dramatic split with Ferrari, a chassis that danced on the limit, and aerodynamic intuition sculpted in a primitive wind tunnel. It was, in essence, the perfect confluence of art and aggression.

Enzo Ferrari famously said, 'The client is not always right.' The 250 GTO reflects that ethos. Buyers weren't just customers – they were chosen. Vetted. Trusted to steward something sacred. Driving a GTO wasn't just about ownership. It was about joining a legacy.

If every Ferrari 250 GTO has its own legend, then chassis #3451GT wears its history like a laurel wreath. Completed on 20 April 1962, this car was the fourth GTO ever assembled. But this wasn't a car meant for display. Within weeks of its birth, it was in Sicily, on the

The incredibly spartan cockpit of a racing car: bare metal everywhere, maximum weight reduction, and the iconic blue fabric seats of Ferrari competition cars.

This 250 GTO was the first to win a European race: the GT class at the 1962 Targa Florio, where its white roof helped reduce cockpit temperatures.

start line of one of motorsport's greatest challenges: the Targa Florio.

Its first owner, the wealthy industrialist and loyal Ferrari customer Pietro Ferraro, understood the heat of competition – quite literally. In preparation for the punishing Mediterranean sun and to cool the cockpit, the *Marrone* (dark brown) body was crowned with a white roof, a striking and unusual decision for a racing Ferrari. On 6 May 1962, Ferraro and his co-driver, Giorgio Scarlatti, crossed the finish line in 4th place overall, clinching victory in the GT class. It was more than a win. It was a coronation and the very first European triumph for a 250 GTO.

What followed was a life lived at speed. After a few less successful outings in Italy, chassis #3451GT was repainted red and passed into the hands of Frenchman Guy Rivillon, who entered it in numerous national rallies. These weren't the most natural battlegrounds for a big front-engined Ferrari, yet it defied expectations, claiming over a dozen additional victories and carving its name even deeper into motorsport history.

Around a decade ago, #3451GT was lovingly restored to its original colours – that deep, rich brown and sun-reflecting white roof – just as it had appeared during its moment of glory on the mountain roads of Sicily.

And that legacy of the Ferrari endures. Today, when a 250 GTO appears – whether on a concours lawn, a historic track, or beside the still waters of Lake Como – time slows. Voices hush. It's not just a car that enters the frame. It's a legend that never left. ■

Engine RPM, water and oil temperature, oil and fuel pressure, fuel level – everything you need to monitor a racing Colombo V12. Speed? Irrelevant. On the track, there are no limits.

86
603
XVM

FERRARI 250 GTO

1962–1964
36 units produced
V12 engine (2,953 cc)
Circa 300 hp
280 km/h

SHELBY COBRA 289

THE SNAKE OVER PARIS

MONTMARTRE, PARIS, FRANCE

GASCOGNE
AU CADET de GASCOGNE
Restaurant salle au 1er

If you've ever heard a Cobra roar to life, this photograph will seem impossibly loud – the walls of old Paris must still be quivering from the ferocious vibrations of its 289 ci V8.

Paris doesn't often echo with thunder. But then again, the Cobra was never built to whisper. On the heights of Montmartre, where painters once traded wine for canvas and poets chased light across stone alleys, a different kind of art now roars to life: British lines, American muscle. A snarling V8 above the city of lights.

This is no museum piece. It's a Shelby Cobra 289, the version that truly carved the Cobra name into motorsport history. It struck a rare balance – ferocious on the track, yet elegant enough to charm the streets of Europe. Compared to the later 427, which was widened, hardened and brutalised for big-block dominance, the 289 retained lithe proportions and razor-sharp responses. It was a driver's machine, not just a missile – and the purest expression of the Shelby vision.

In the early 1960s, Carroll Shelby had a simple dream: take the nimble AC Ace chassis and shove in a small-block Ford V8, initially a 260 cubic inch unit, but soon upgraded to 289 cubic inches (4.7 litres). What emerged wasn't just a car – it was a declaration. The 289 kept the finesse of the original British roadster but infused it with raw, American purpose.

Power output climbed from 275 horsepower in early street models to well over 385 in race-prepared variants – numbers that, in a chassis weighing just over 900 kg, meant pure adrenaline. The zero to 100 km/h sprint? Under five seconds. Top speed? North of 240 km/h, depending on gearing and set-up.

But the Cobra wasn't just about brute force. Rack-and-pinion steering replaced the worm-and-sector system of the AC Ace, giving it precision to match its punch. The suspension remained fully independent, with transverse leaf springs: an old-school set-up, but tuned for agility. Disc brakes all around kept things in check, though just barely at racing speeds.

This was the car that carried Shelby to the 1965 FIA GT Manufacturers' Championship, beating Ferrari at its own game. With drivers like Ken Miles and Bob Bondurant at the wheel, the 289 Cobra earned victories at Nassau, Sebring, Goodwood and beyond. It was the underdog with a Texan snarl and a British backbone.

The green example seen here, gleaming against the backdrop of Parisian sky, is a street car, but only just. Big exhaust pipes, Halibrand-style knock-off wheels and the unmistakable stance suggest a machine still restless, still hungry.

Its chassis number? #CSX2493. Born in England on 23 June 1964, it was assembled at the AC works in Thames Ditton before crossing the Atlantic to Shelby's

LA MERE CATHERINE
LA MERE CATHERINE
LA MERE CATHERINE
BAR
BRASSERIE
JARDIN ET BOSQUET
SALON DE THE
DG700LL

A massive 4.7-litre V8, four oversized wheels, a frail body draped over the mechanics, and a stripped-down cockpit for the driver: this is the Cobra, a car where power is the only thing that truly matters.

According to legend, the name 'Cobra' came to Carroll Shelby in a dream.

Born in England as the discreet AC Ace, the Cobra flexed its muscles once it crossed to America!

Los Angeles base, where its Ford V8 heart was installed in early July. Originally delivered in white with a black interior, it spent nearly a year waiting for its first owner – Lewis Downs, a Californian hi-fi specialist and hot rod enthusiast who didn't waste time making it his own. Out went the original wire wheels, replaced by oversized rims that demanded wider arches and a more aggressive stance.

By the end of 1966, Downs had traded road noise for roadies, selling the car to Tom Barbour, a devoted Shelby club member and autocross competitor. Barbour saw a beast waiting to be unleashed. Special heads, wild cams and even more pronounced fenders were fitted. The Cobra was reborn in a striking Cadillac hue – *Light Firemist Green* – and campaigned hard from 1967 until 1970. Then, silence. For 36 years, it sat dormant.

In 2006, it returned to life. Fully restored and soon shipped to France, it wore a brief disguise in white and red as it roared through historic racing events, powered by a 400-horsepower engine.

Now, it stands once more in green, glowing softly against Parisian stone, its red leather interior catching the last of the evening light. A Cobra with decades of character in its wake. No replica, no tribute – this is the real deal, shaped by speed, scars, and the dreams of California's golden age. And here it is, above Montmartre. A growl among rooftops. A ghost with traction.

But maybe it fits. Paris has always been a city of dualities. Beauty and revolution. Elegance and upheaval. Marble façades and burning barricades. It knows how to welcome the radical, how to fold noise into art. And now, thunder on the hill – a snarling V8 beneath the shadow of the Sacré-Cœur, echoing through streets where chansons once floated. The Cobra may be foreign, loud, defiant. But so, too, was every movement that ever reshaped this city. It doesn't clash. It belongs. ■

internet

SHELBY COBRA 289

1963–1965
About 528 units produced
V8 engine (4,737 cc)
From 275 hp
220 km/h

1965

FORD GT40

THE HEART AND SOUL OF SHELBY AMERICAN

SOUTH KENSINGTON, LONDON, GREAT BRITAIN

FORD

APO 227C

An uncommon sight: a Ford GT40 Mk I on the streets of London, a true racing thoroughbred far from its natural habitat. Built with a single purpose – to conquer the 24 Hours of Le Mans – the GT40 would go on to deliver Ford four consecutive victories between 1966 and 1969.

It's a strange sort of poetry: the Ford GT40, born of rivalry and American muscle, prowling the narrow, cobbled lanes of old London. Between brick courtyards and soot-stained façades, its low, brooding stance looks less like a visitor and more like a weapon biding its time. Maroon paint catching just enough of the city's grey light to feel royal, almost regal. But this is no ceremonial car. It was built to destroy kings.

The GT40 didn't begin as a racing car. It began as an act of revenge. After Enzo Ferrari walked away from Ford's acquisition attempt in 1963, Henry Ford II didn't just vow to beat Ferrari – he promised to humiliate them where it hurt most: Le Mans. He hired Eric Broadley of Lola, tapped Carroll Shelby's brilliance and poured millions into an audacious idea: to create an American car capable of dethroning Europe's racing elite.

And it worked. Painfully at first, gloriously in the end. The GT40 would go on to win Le Mans four years in a row, from 1966 to 1969, etching itself into motorsport legend with a thunderous V8 and the silhouette of a low-slung brawler.

The Mk I, the foundation of the dynasty, was a transatlantic hybrid. Its chassis came from Eric Broadley's Lola Mk6: a steel monocoque, light but sturdy, revolutionary for its time. To this, Ford added its own power: a 4.7-litre (289 cubic inch) V8, borrowed from the Shelby Cobra. Simple in theory. But what mattered was the way it was tuned – dry-sumped, mid-mounted and fed by four Weber carburettors. The result was around 380 horsepower pushing just over 1,000 kg of mass.

Performance was visceral. Top speed flirted with 320 km/h. Zero to 60 mph in the low four seconds. But the magic wasn't straight-line – it was stability. That impossibly low height, just 40 inches from ground to roof, gave it the centre of gravity of a jet-fuelled ant. Combined with wind-tunnel-developed aerodynamics, it planted itself on the tarmac at speed. Calm. Ruthless.

Inside? Nothing superfluous. Just rivets, switches and fatigue. The driving position was skewed to the centre, pedals offset, noise omnipresent. But to those who understood, it felt like a cockpit, not a compromise.

Only 87 Mk I chassis were built. Of those, a fraction were road-registered. Even fewer survived intact. Each one is an artefact of war: machine as declaration, steel as strategy. An homologation car built with just enough civility to wear plates, but every inch a racer underneath. It rides barely a metre high. Doors cut into the roof for clearance. Gears that clunk with mechanical truth. And a cabin so tight it feels more like being strapped inside a warhead than seated in a grand tourer.

This car, chassis #P/1018, tells a story not just of racing, but of theatre. One of only two GT40s constructed

A name that says it all: GT40 – for 40 inches high, barely more than a metre from the ground!

FORD
GOODYEAR
GOODYEAR

Raw power: mounted in a mid-rear position, the robust 4.7-litre Ford V8 delivers close to 400 horsepower.

The door opens with a section of the roof itself, a clever solution to ease access for the helmeted driver.

to racing spec for promotional duties, it was personally commissioned by Carroll Shelby in a deep, elegant maroon over black leather – an unusual choice that made it stand out even in stillness. It was also the first GT40 to feature the distinctive three-hole chassis panel. Shipped to California in November 1965, it posed proudly for photographs at Shelby's Los Angeles Airport workshop before embarking on a car shows tour through Seattle, San Francisco and Portland. Curiously, Shelby only ever drove two GT40s himself, and this was one of them.

Its next role came on the big screen. In 1966, it was handed to Bob Bondurant for high-speed camera tests at Riverside Raceway, part of the pre-production for John Frankenheimer's *Grand Prix*. Soon after, it wore a coat of blue and slipped into television, appearing in an episode of *The Man from U.N.C.L.E.* before being sold in 1968. Its journey took it to the garage of British racer David Piper, then to Australia, then Japan. In 2001, it was bought by endurance veteran Ray Bellm, who finally returned it to what it was built for: racing. Historic grids followed, along with a turn on *Top Gear*, where the car showed it hadn't lost its voice. Today, restored to its original maroon, #P/1018 stands as a testament to the show and the substance of Ford's boldest machine.

And yet, here it is, echoing off Georgian walls and Victorian iron, softer somehow in the silence of South Kensington's backstreets. A monument not just to speed, but to pride, obsession, and the kind of stubborn ambition that rewrites history. Not all icons wear crowns. Some wear scars. And a set of magnesium wheels. ■

GOODYEAR

FORD GT40

1964–1965
87 units produced (31 street cars)
V8 engine (4,737 cc)
380 hp (335 hp in street version)
Around 320 km/h

1965

ASTON MARTIN DB5 'BOND CAR'

IN THE FOOTSTEPS OF 007

FURKA PASS, SWITZERLAND

BMT 216A

This is no costume, no replica: this Aston Martin DB5 is one of only four built at the time to the exact specifications of the film *Goldfinger*, for Eon Productions, the company behind the James Bond movies.

It's the most famous car in the world. The machine that defined not just a brand, but an entire cinematic mythology. And here, on the winding sweep of the Furka Pass, fiction folds into reality once more.

This particular Aston Martin DB5 isn't just a lookalike. Chassis #DB5/2008/R was purchased new by Eon Productions in 1965 for the promotion of *Thunderball*, fresh off the global success of *Goldfinger*, where the silver coupe first slipped into immortality. Used in official photographs and press tours, it quickly became one of the most visible ambassadors of Bond's new automotive identity.

But what makes it more than a piece of promotional memorabilia is where it returns today. The Furka Pass – those switchbacks suspended above the Rhône Glacier – was the actual filming location for one of *Goldfinger*'s most iconic scenes. Sean Connery, ice-cool behind the wheel, machine guns tucked into the headlights, a DB5 dancing along the spine of the Alps like a weaponised ballerina. To honour that cinematic moment, we returned at the same time of year the film was shot, chasing the same alpine light that once lit 007's path. A scene not recreated, but relived.

Fifty years later, the same wind sweeps across the peaks. The same rock faces echo the sound of a straight-six engine climbing through the revs. A kind of cinematic déjà vu – except this time, it's real.

The DB5 didn't arrive with a bang. It emerged quietly, an evolution rather than a revolution. But that's always been the Aston Martin way: refinement over reinvention.

Beneath the timeless shape, it was born from the bones of the DB4 Series V, sharing its Superleggera construction – aluminium panels stretched over a tubular frame – but with subtle, telling upgrades. The most important was under the bonnet: a bored-out version of Tadek Marek's inline-six, now at 4.0 litres, delivering 282 horsepower in standard trim. That meant more torque, smoother delivery and better high-speed composure.

It gained sophistication, too. A new ZF five-speed gearbox replaced the old four-speed unit. Servo-assisted Girling disc brakes offered stronger, more consistent stops. Electric windows, twin fuel tanks and even optional air conditioning added a level of civility few GTs of the day could match.

Visually, the DB5 kept its predecessor's poise but gained just enough presence. Subtly flared arches, revised tail lamps and a slightly wider stance gave it the gravitas to match its newfound fame.

BMT 216A

No ordinary dashboard: tucked beneath the armrest, a suite of switches allows James Bond to activate the various gadgets of his DB5 – would you be able to resist the temptation?

The DB5 wasn't just a faster DB4. It was something rarer: a car that had matured without losing its spirit. The same suit, but tailored sharper, cut from finer cloth. It elevated the DB4 in every way. Luxurious but fast. Elegant but dangerous. The perfect Bond, in car form.

This car – chassis #DB5/2008/R – wasn't seen on screen in a Bond movie, but it was every bit the star. One of two identical DB5s commissioned by Eon Productions to promote *Thunderball* in the United States, it shared every gadget with Bond's on-screen ride, and arguably did it better.

Unlike the quickly improvised props built by the film crew, this car's arsenal was fitted directly by Aston Martin, engineered for durability and function. And function they still do: front and rear hydraulic rams hidden in the bumpers, Browning .30-calibre machine guns in the fenders, tyre slashers at the wheel hubs, a retractable bulletproof rear shield, oil-slick and smokescreen dispensers, a radar scope in the dash, revolving licence plates, even the iconic passenger ejection system – all intact, all operational.

Sold by Eon in 1969 to famed British collector Anthony Bamford, 2008/R remained in his care before crossing the Atlantic to an American museum, where it spent 35 quiet years on display – its gadgets resting, but ready – until returning to the road in 2006.

Only four DB5s were built to *Goldfinger* specification in-period, and this is one of them. A real-deal Q-Branch creation. A monument not just to Aston Martin, but to cinema history.

Back then, it was an aspirational fantasy. Today, it's an artefact. A time machine on wire wheels. Standing here, in the very curve where fiction became legend, it still wears that role with effortless grace. ■

The engine rooms: up front, the 4.0-litre straight-six Aston Martin; at the rear, the compressed air, nitrogen and hydraulic systems that power the car's various gadgets on screen, filling the entire boot space.

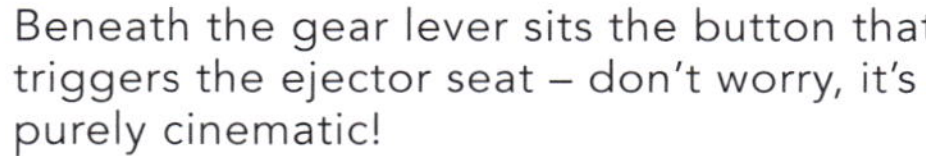
Beneath the gear lever sits the button that triggers the ejector seat – don't worry, it's purely cinematic!

The machine guns are retractable tubes connected to oxygen and acetylene canisters, spitting sparks that look startlingly real.

BMT 216A

ASTON MARTIN DB5 'BOND CAR'

1963–1965
1,059 units produced
Straight-six engine (3,996 cc)
282 hp
230 km/h

1967

ALFA ROMEO 33 STRADALE

BLUE JEWEL OF THE BISCIONE

CANTON OF ZURICH, SWITZERLAND

It might be the most beautiful car ever designed, and the only one that was ever painted blue. A rare vision: no one has had the chance to photograph it outdoors for decades.

You don't expect to find a spaceship parked quietly among the hills of Zurich canton. But that's exactly what this feels like. A ripple of pure design. A hallucination on magnesium wheels. The Alfa Romeo 33 Stradale is so rare, so sculpturally perfect, that it seems implausible it was ever meant for the road. And this one – painted a deep, royal blue – is the only one of its kind.

The Alfa Romeo 33 Stradale was not just a sports car, but a declaration. A brief, glorious moment when Alfa Romeo turned its back on compromise and built something irrational, extraordinary and utterly pure. Born directly from the crucible of motorsport, the Stradale was based on the Tipo 33 prototype – a closed-cockpit racing car developed by Alfa's Autodelta division under the leadership of Carlo Chiti. That bloodline is not a romantic metaphor: it shares its chassis, suspension and even engine architecture with Alfa's endurance racers.

At the centre of the 33 Stradale's perfection lies its 2.0-litre V8, a dry-sump, 90-degree jewel with twin overhead camshafts per bank and fuel injection. The engine revved to nearly 10,000 rpm – a sonic rarity on public roads – and produced approximately 230 horsepower, though some estimates place it closer to 250. Given the car's featherweight build, weighing just 700 kg thanks to a magnesium and aluminium body over a tubular spaceframe, it delivered a power-to-weight ratio that would embarrass cars made decades later. Zero to 100 km/h took under six seconds, and top speed approached 260 km/h, staggering figures for 1967.

But the numbers tell only part of the story. The 33 Stradale was built like a racing car because it was one. The chassis, officially known as the Tipo 33/2, featured a fully independent suspension with unequal-length double wishbones and inboard disc brakes all around. The butterfly doors were not a stylistic flourish, but a practical solution to the car's low roofline and tall sills. Even the glass canopy was designed with airflow and visibility in mind.

VA-24
2413

Part of the 33 Stradale's mesmerising beauty lies in its incredibly delicate butterfly doors, carrying a portion of the glass roof with them. When the demands of competition give birth to a masterpiece.

One of the most exquisite jewels to grace an automotive body: the Alfa Romeo scudetto.

Could you resist the invitation to step into this mechanical monument?

Its form was entrusted to Franco Scaglione, arguably one of the greatest visionaries in automotive design. Scaglione gave the 33 Stradale its ethereal curves and impossible stance, a blend of aerodynamic logic and sensual grace. It looked fast standing still. It looked alive. Many consider it the most beautiful car ever built – not just by Alfa, but by anyone.

Only 18 chassis were constructed between 1967 and 1969, and no two were exactly the same. Several were later used as the basis for Alfa's radical concept cars – of the road-going cars, only a handful survived in completely original condition.

The car you see here – chassis #75033.111 – is unlike any other. Specially commissioned by Corrado Agusta, heir to the MV Agusta empire, it stands alone in the Stradale family. While most wore racing red, Agusta chose a rich royal blue, with a brown and blue interior – a palette more yacht than prototype, more Riviera than racetrack.

But the individuality ran deeper than colour. Finding the standard seats too pedestrian, Agusta replaced them with Agusta helicopter seats, complete with Volvo-sourced seatbelts. He added an ashtray between them – because even in a car that redlines at 10,000 rpm, one might want a cigarette – and requested a dual

The minimalist dashboard is a reminder that, above all, this is a tool for a race driver.

A unique detail marking its first owner: the seats were sourced from an Agusta helicopter.

brake-assist system to tame the Stradale's fierce disc brakes. It was a rolling manifesto of style, eccentricity and engineering precision.

Years later, it crossed continents into a Japanese collection, where it was repainted red, perhaps to blend in. But such a car was never meant to disappear. When it returned to Europe, it underwent a painstaking 5,000-hour restoration, reclaiming its original colours and quirks. Today, it is once again exactly as Corrado Agusta imagined it: utterly, gloriously unique.

And now, here it is, under the soft light of the Zurich countryside. A car born of Italian passion, shaped by aviation eccentricity and weathered by decades of quiet exile, back in the heart of Europe. Among the gentle hills and tiled farmhouses, it looks almost surreal – otherworldly in its shimmer, yet undeniably present.

What makes this moment even more extraordinary is its rarity: no one had photographed this very car in the open air for decades. Hidden away in private hands, it had become a ghost – whispered about, but seldom seen. And yet here it stands, the only blue 33 Stradale ever made. The only one like it in the world. And, for a fleeting moment, ours alone to witness. ■

Anything but a road engine: Alfa Romeo's 2.0-litre V8 revs to 10,000 rpm, screaming with a spine-tingling ferocity.

ALFA ROMEO 33 STRADALE

1967–1969
18 units produced (including the concept cars)
V8 engine (1,995 cc)
230 hp
260 km/h

1968

DE TOMASO MANGUSTA

COBRA KILLER IN COUTURE

PLACE VENDÔME, PARIS, FRANCE

The most spectacular detail of the Mangusta's stunning bodywork: its twin rear hatches opening like butterfly wings, a dramatic flourish reminiscent of pre-war grand tourers. Practical? Perhaps not. Stylish? Absolutely.

It shouldn't work. A snarling V8 brute in the middle of Paris's most refined square. Burgundy paint glinting under the wrought-iron balconies of the Ritz. But it does. The De Tomaso Mangusta has the rare ability to look at home among tailored suits and champagne flutes while also suggesting it might tear the whole place apart.

Alejandro De Tomaso never built cars to play nice. The Mangusta was his act of defiance – against Carroll Shelby, against convention, against the safe idea of what a sports car should be. The name said it all: *mangusta*, meaning mongoose, the natural enemy of the cobra. After a proposed mid-engined collaboration with Shelby collapsed in the mid-1960s, De Tomaso went ahead and built it anyway. The result wasn't a compromise. It was a weapon.

From that origin came one of the most provocative shapes ever put on the road. Designed by a young Giorgetto Giugiaro during his time at Ghia, the Mangusta wasn't about flow or grace, but about tension. A blade-thin centre section stretched between muscular fenders. A sharp nose free of any bumper. A rear deck that opened in butterfly fashion, twin panels lifting to reveal the beast within.

That beast was a 4.7-litre Ford V8, mounted behind the cabin and paired to a five-speed ZF transaxle. With over 300 horsepower on tap, it wasn't just quick – it was raw. The power delivery was instant, the engine note guttural. The chassis, borrowed from De Tomaso's earlier racing efforts, was rigid and nimble, but not forgiving. The steering was unassisted, the pedals offset, the visibility nearly non-existent. Driving it was an act of physical intent. Parking it? A performance art.

But what a performance. With its cast magnesium Campagnolo wheels, quadruple headlights hidden beneath eyelids, and impossibly low profile – just 43 inches at the roof – the Mangusta was pure cinematic attitude. The interior was trimmed in black vinyl and brushed aluminium, more fighter jet than grand tourer. Storage was nearly non-existent, ergonomics an afterthought. It didn't care. That wasn't the point.

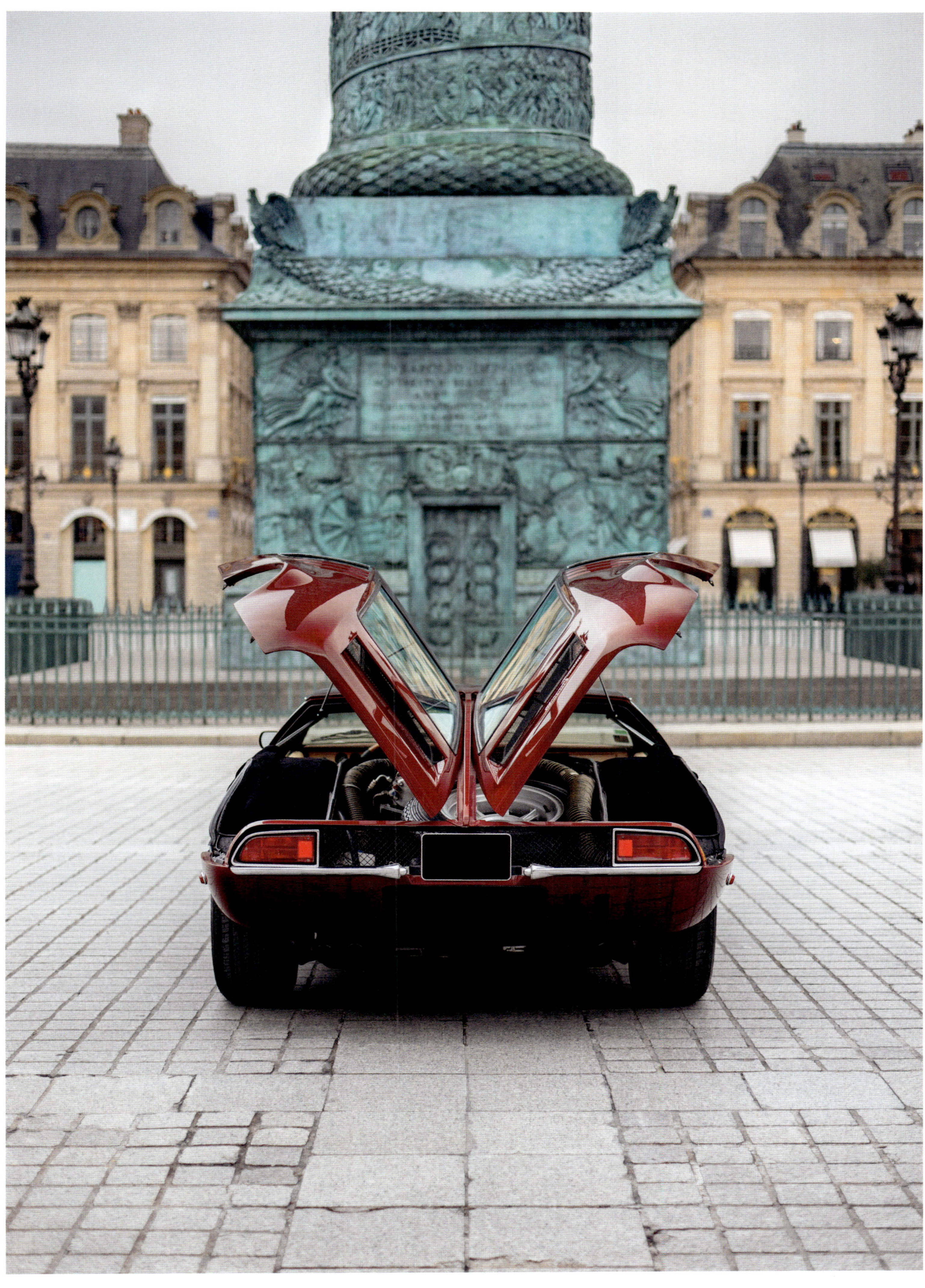

A horizontal, no-frills layout of the instruments – so typical of many GTs from the late 1960s and early 1970s – yet this particular Mangusta stands out with a far more joyful presentation than most of its kind.

Only 401 Mangustas were ever built between 1967 and 1971, and each one was a bit different. De Tomaso's factory in Modena was small, flexible and chaotic. Details changed without warning. Some cars had power windows, others did not. Some had two wipers, others three. Fit and finish depended on the day of the week. But each car shared the same DNA: provocative lines, brutal mechanics and a total disinterest in compromise.

This 1968 example, painted a rich, deep burgundy that glows against the limestone façades of the square, is the Mangusta at its most refined. Subtle in colour but outrageous in shape, it reflects the duality that defines the car: a sculpture of speed that was built to scare its driver. A fashion statement with the soul of a fistfight.

This is chassis #798, built in late 1968 for the American market and powered by the 302 cubic inch Ford V8 (European cars featured the 289 ci engine), paired with a five-speed ZF manual gearbox. Finished in this deep, burnished shade of brown, it was delivered that November to importer Kjell Qvale Motorcars in California, complete with factory air conditioning and a standard black vinyl interior. Only after its arrival in France in 2012 did the car undergo a transformation –

Beneath the twin-opening rear deck of this Mangusta lies the 4.9-litre V8 reserved for the American versions.

And the name says it all: *mangusta* – the mongoose – born with one clear mission, to strike at the Cobra!

its cabin reupholstered in pale beige leather of striking refinement, bringing an unmistakable touch of couture to an already sculptural machine.

De Tomaso would go on to build more successful cars. But never a purer one. The Mangusta was lightning in a bottle: raw ambition cast in steel and aluminium, wearing Giugiaro's sharpest suit. It demanded attention, demanded skill and demanded space. And all these years later, it still does.

At Place Vendôme, where the weight of history lingers in the shadows of colonnades and gilded façades, the Mangusta doesn't shout. It suggests. Like a guest at an haute couture salon who wasn't expected, yet steals every glance. There's something about its stance – low, poised, uncompromising – that fits among the Parisian codes of elegance while gently subverting them. Not a relic, but a reminder: true style isn't about fitting in. It's about refusing to. ■

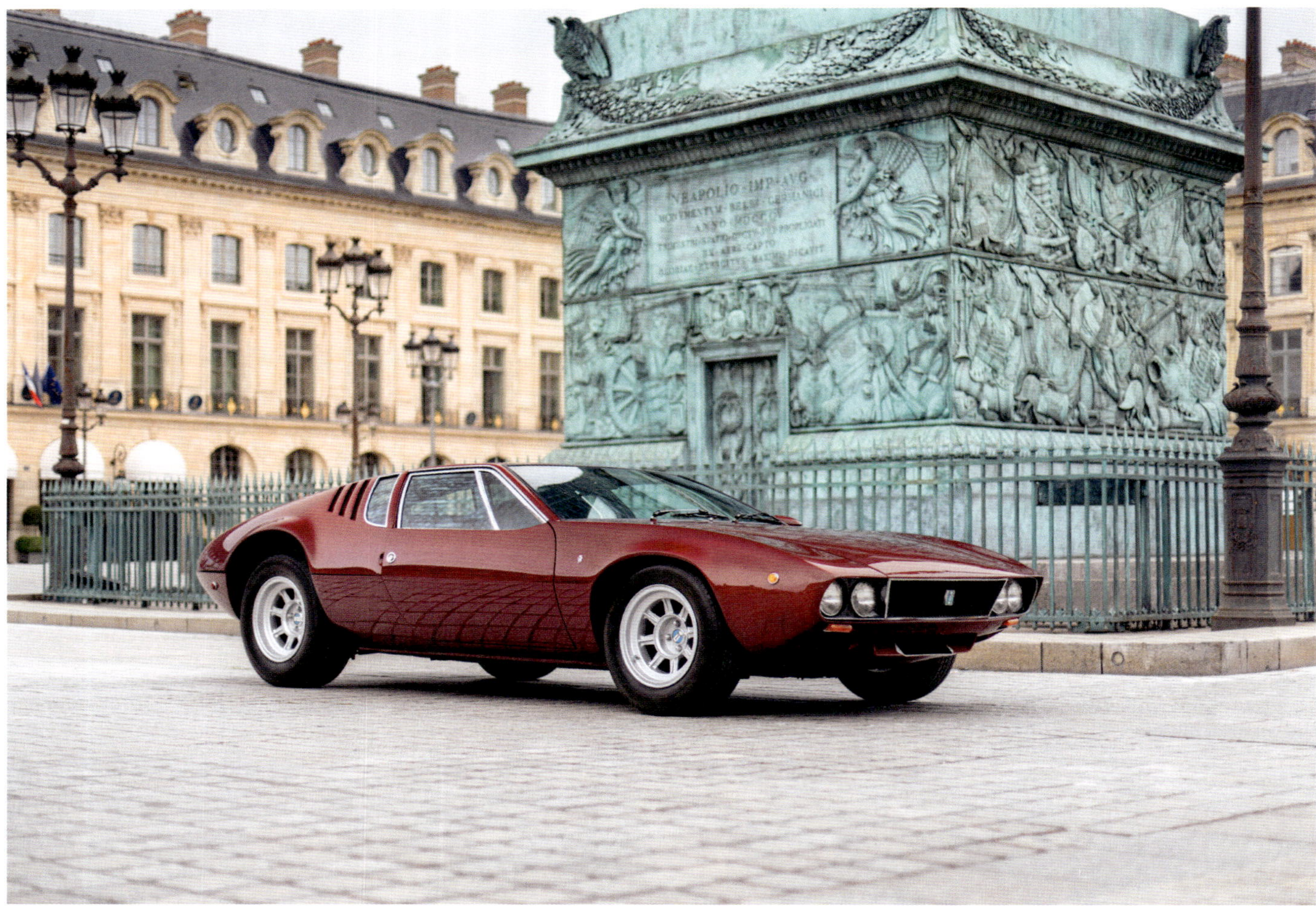

The unmistakable touch of designer Giorgetto Giugiaro: a style less sculptural, more pared-down, with perfectly balanced proportions – foreshadowing the more industrial design language that would soon define the automobile.

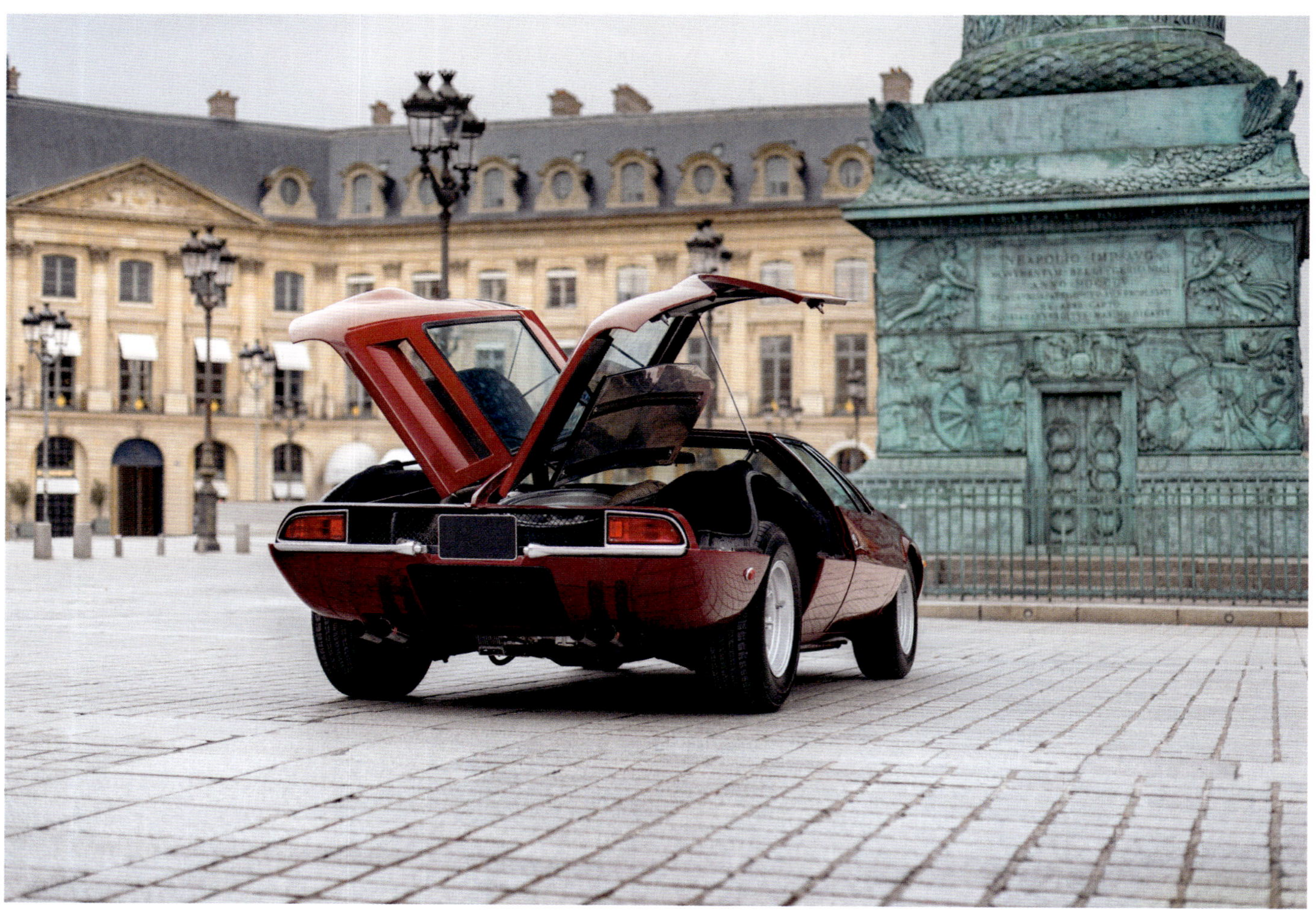

DE TOMASO MANGUSTA

1967–1971
401 units produced
V8 engine (4,942 cc)
230 hp
250 km/h

ALPINE A220

FROM MULSANNE TO THE MÉTRO

PLACE DE LA CONCORDE, PARIS, FRANCE

4517 GN 76
elf

A Le Mans prototype, complete with a licence plate, right in the heart of Paris? Yes, this endurance Alpine was modified to tackle road rallies as well.

It's a strange feeling to see a Le Mans prototype idle between taxis and tour buses in the heart of Paris. Place de la Concorde is a stage of history: kings fell here, revolutions spun their wheels. But this is no ordinary car. This is an Alpine A220. A Le Mans prototype that, against all odds, found its way to the capital of France.

Born from ambition and crafted in the shadows of Dieppe's workshops, the A220 was Alpine's boldest creation. In the mid-1960s, Jean Rédélé had already made a name with lightweight, agile cars that danced on alpine passes and dominated rally stages. But Le Mans was different. It was war at 300 km/h. To fight it, Alpine needed something radical.

The A220 was the culmination of that effort. Designed around a tubular spaceframe chassis, it featured a mid-mounted 3.0-litre V8 engine developed with Gordini – compact, naturally aspirated and capable of revving past 8,000 rpm. Fibreglass bodywork kept the weight under 800 kg, while aerodynamic experimentation gave rise to the car's distinctive long tail, crafted to cheat the wind on the Mulsanne Straight.

In 1968 and 1969, Alpine entered multiple A220s in the 24 Hours of Le Mans. Though beautiful and brave, the cars were plagued by reliability issues and a lack of outright speed compared to Ferrari, Ford and Porsche. Still, they represented the highest expression of French racing pride at the time: purpose-built machines that carried national hopes at La Sarthe.

Only a handful of A220s were built – just nine cars, including the A222 and A223 variations – and none were meant for life beyond the pit lane. Except one.

Chassis #1731 began as all A220s did – on the starting grid, with ambition in its veins and Le Mans in its sights. Campaigned by Alpine's factory team, it saw action in a string of high-profile endurance events: the 500 km of Zeltweg, the 1,000 km of Spa, The Grand Prix de la Corniche in Morocco, and twice at the 24 Hours of Le Mans (1968 and '69). Its finest moment came at the 1,000 km of Paris in 1968, where it crossed the line in 4th place – respectable, if not revolutionary. The rest of its racing résumé reads like a tale of near misses and mechanical misfortunes. Glorious failure, by another name.

But its story didn't end with retirement. Instead, #1731 was reborn. The original long tail was cut down to sharpen its reflexes. The engine and suspension were reworked for better balance. And then, most astonishingly, it was registered for the road, becoming the only A220 ever to receive such approval. A full-blown prototype, with licence plates.

4517 GN 76

A view that leaves no doubt: the tail of this endurance prototype was truncated for greater agility in rallies. Under the bonnet, it still houses the 3.0-litre Gordini V8.

A typical circuit prototype layout: right-hand drive to place the driver closest to the apex on tracks that most often run clockwise.

The finest French drivers of the era took the wheel of this car: Jean Guichet, already a seasoned veteran, alongside others who would go on to become legends.

Its second life proved just as adventurous. Now in hill climb trim, it was driven by Jean Vinatier to a 3rd-place finish at Chamrousse in 1969 and a 2nd-place podium at the Nogaro Grand Prix. But its final competition outing, the Critérium des Cévennes that same year, ended in familiar fashion: a DNF for Jean-Pierre Jabouille. After that, silence.

The car passed into private hands, those of a former Alpine employee who spent more than twenty years restoring it with respect and precision. Eventually, it emerged again. Not as a replica, not as a showpiece, but as what it had always been: a machine that lived at full throttle, now with stories etched into every curve.

It's strange and wonderful, seeing it here. This once-nervous racer with a five-speed gearbox and four Weber carburettors, slinking between pedestrians on Place de la Concorde. An arena of revolution and royalty. But the car doesn't feel out of place.

Today, it still wears its shortened body and remains remarkably intact. Its fibreglass panels barely contain its racing origins: ventilated four-wheel disc brakes, inboard rear suspension, wide magnesium wheels. No luxuries. No concessions. Just race engineering in raw, elegant form.

And maybe that's the point. The A220 was never a success. It was too pure. Too focused. But #1731 escaped. It was reborn. From La Sarthe to the pavement cafés of Paris, it bridges two worlds: racer and road car, memory and motion. ■

elf
J. GUICHET J.P. JABOUILLE (LM 68)
J.P. NICOLAS J.L. THERIER (LM 69)

ALPINE A220

1968–1969
8 units produced
V8 engine (2,986 cc)
310 hp
330 km/h

1968

LAMBORGHINI MIURA ROADSTER

THE RAREST BULL

CANTON OF ZURICH, SWITZERLAND

The Miura had already taken the sports car world by storm with its uncompromising silhouette and, above all, its mid-mounted engine. Yet Lamborghini still had some surprises in store, unveiling a spectacular roadster that would remain forever unique.

It looked like the future. Not the orderly, functional future imagined by engineers and bureaucrats, but the untamed future dreamt of by poets and rebels. When Lamborghini unveiled the Miura in 1966, it wasn't just a car. It was an explosion of shape and sound, a kind of automotive revolution that caught even Ferrari flat-footed.

Mid-engined, with a transversely mounted V12 and a chassis derived from racing prototypes, the Miura was unlike anything that had come before it. It was a street-legal exotic with a racing soul – elegant, impossible, wildly fast. And yet its story was born not in boardrooms but in backrooms.

Three men, all in their 20s – Giampaolo Dallara, Paolo Stanzani and Bob Wallace – conspired after hours at Lamborghini's Sant'Agata factory. Dallara shaped the steel backbone chassis; Stanzani engineered the complex mechanics; Wallace made sure it handled like nothing else on the road. They brought the idea to Ferruccio Lamborghini, who reluctantly gave his blessing. Design duties went to the young Marcello Gandini at Bertone, who sculpted a shape that seemed to defy time and gravity alike.

What emerged at the 1966 Geneva Motor Show was an icon born fully formed. The Miura was compact, lithe, with hips like Brigitte Bardot and eyes like a hunting cat. Underneath: a 3.9-litre V12 producing around 350 horsepower, mounted transversely just behind the seats. The gearbox and engine shared a crankcase. It was both masterpiece and madness. The world had never seen anything like it.

And yet, just two years later, Lamborghini did something even more audacious.

At the 1968 Brussels Motor Show, nestled between staid sedans and clunky saloons, sat a vision: the Miura Roadster. Painted in a hypnotic pale metallic blue – *Lamè Sky Blu* – with an ivory white and dark red interior and no roof at all, it stunned everyone. A convertible supercar that still looked impossibly pure, even without the iconic roofline.

But this was no quick chop job. Bertone, with Gandini again at the pen, had reimagined the Miura as an open-top sculpture. The windshield was lower and raked more steeply, and there were no side windows. The rear buttresses were reshaped for elegance and air flow. The engine cover was redesigned to flow with the new proportions, and even the roll bar was subtly blended into the curvature of the bodywork. Finally, the steering wheel was the same type as that of the Lamborghini Marzal concept car. It retained the 4.0-litre V12 – 380 horsepower in its latest tune – and a top speed near 280 km/h, though no one really cared. What mattered was how it looked. And it looked divine.

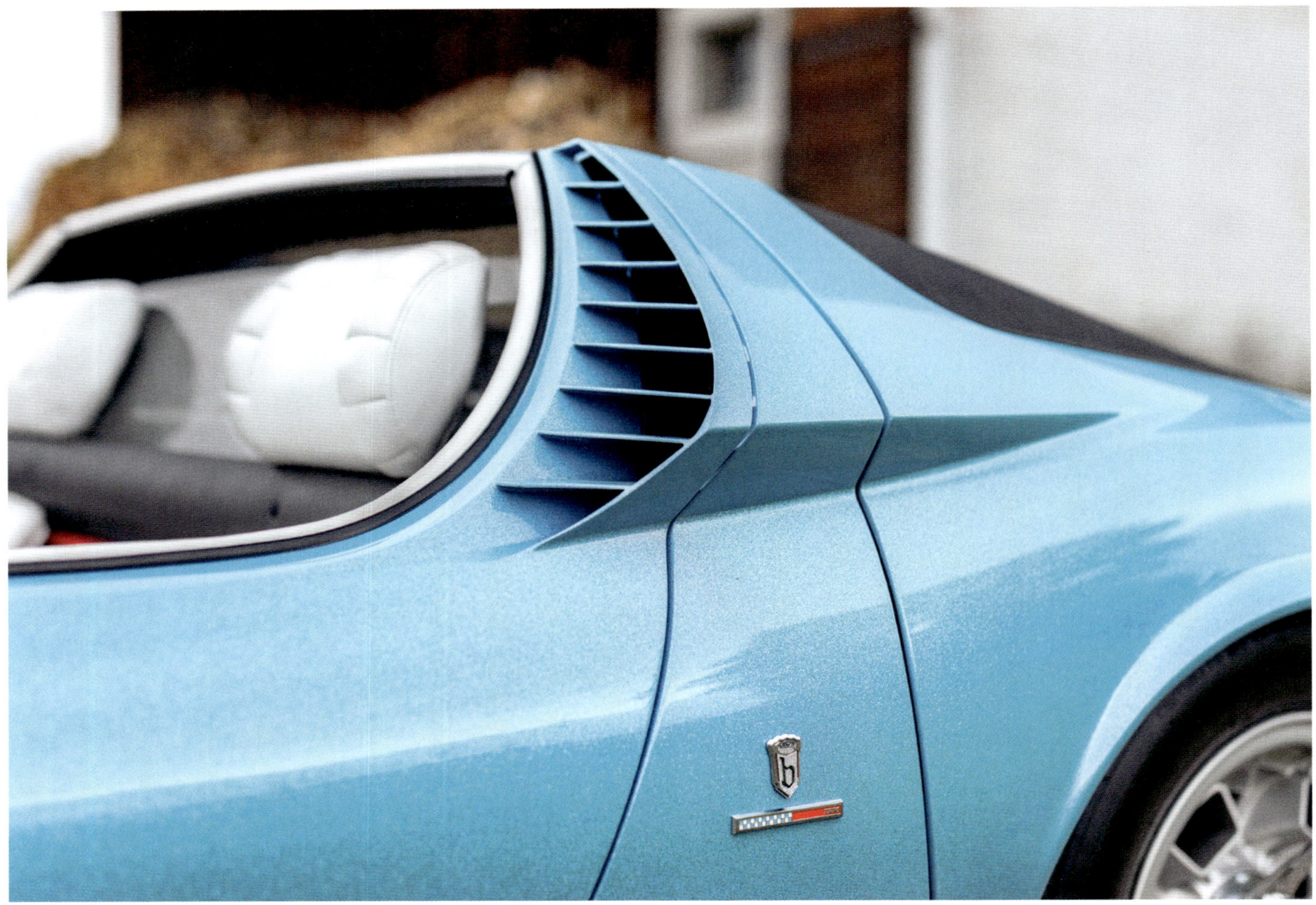

All the iconic details of the Miura are there, like the eyelash-like headlight trims, which helped build the Miura's legend, yet with an even more distinctive flair – most notably in the reshaped air intakes, giving this one-off its own unmistakable identity.

CARELLO

MIURA roadster
Lamborghini Bertone

The original Lamborghini V12 enjoyed an incredible lifespan of nearly 50 years, yet its transverse layout remained unique to the Miura. On this car, the rear bonnet was redesigned: it is the only Miura with the engine exposed.

But Ferruccio Lamborghini, ever the pragmatist, said no. He worried that an open-top Miura would compromise the chassis rigidity – or cannibalise sales of the standard coupe. Only this one car was built, never intended for production.

Soon after, the one-off was sold to the International Lead Zinc Research Organization (ILZRO), who had a strange plan for the masterpiece. They renamed it the 'ZN75' and refitted it with experimental zinc-based components – zinc trim, zinc-plated engine parts, and an iridescent golden-green paint job to match. The purpose? To demonstrate the potential of zinc in automotive applications. For years, the Miura Roadster travelled to trade shows and technology exhibitions, a sort of exotic ambassador for industrial metallurgy.

And then, it vanished. It wasn't until decades later that collectors tracked it down – tired, modified, its iconic shape dulled by time and function. But the bones were intact. The car was entrusted to Gary Bobileff, the renowned Miura restorer in California, who embarked on a no-compromise restoration that took thousands of hours and a team of obsessive craftsmen. Every unique detail was researched and replicated, from the slightly altered air intakes to the special brightwork and interior trim. Even the original paint code was matched using archival photos and microscopic paint samples.

The result is the car you see here. On the quiet country roads of the Zurich canton, far from the roaring show floor of Brussels or the fluorescent glare of industrial fairs, the Miura Roadster seems impossibly alive. Its pale blue curves shimmer against the alpine air. There is no roof, no protection; just you, the engine and the horizon.

A Miura was never ordinary. But this one – chassis #3498, the one and only Roadster – is something else entirely. It's not just a car. It's a singular dream, made real. ■

LAMBORGHINI

The *Lamè Sky Blu* and glitter paint dazzles with brilliance, while the raging bull emblem finds its origin in Ferruccio Lamborghini's astrological sign.

LAMBORGHINI MIURA ROADSTER

1968
One-off
V12 engine (3,929 cc)
350 hp
280 km/h

ALFA ROMEO CARABO

FLASH FORWARD

ARESE, METROPOLITAN CITY OF MILAN, ITALY

The shape of things to come: the wedge design that would dominate automotive forms in the 1970s was born with the Alfa Romeo Carabo, a true milestone in automotive design.

The Carabo is one of those cars most people only ever see under glass, if at all. Jealously kept in the Alfa Romeo Museum in Arese, it's more relic than automobile. A flash of late-1960s futurism preserved in metallic green and iridescent orange, like an exotic insect trapped in amber.

The Carabo was not simply a stylistic exercise – it was a manifesto. A 30-year-old Marcello Gandini, then chief designer at Bertone, created something that felt less like a car and more like an object beamed in from another dimension, right after his other revolution – the Lamborghini Miura. Where the curvaceous lines of the 1960s had celebrated sensuality – think Ferrari 275, Jaguar E-Type – the Carabo rejected softness entirely. It was radical geometry: sharp angles, slashes of colour, flat planes and impossible proportions. It didn't look fast. It looked interstellar.

Its front end was a solid, unbroken wedge, with no grille or conventional headlights, just a band of retractable polycarbonate panels that flipped up to reveal slim lamps hidden beneath. The windscreen was almost horizontal, its rake so severe it blended seamlessly into the low-slung roofline. From the side, the car was barely a metre tall, with a beltline that ran dead straight and high across the windows – more spaceship than coupe. The tail was abruptly chopped off, as if sliced with a blade, and punctuated with slatted fins and a glowing orange mesh grille.

But it was the doors that made the biggest impression. The scissor-style hinges, pivoting upwards like a praying mantis ready to strike, had never been seen before on a road car. They weren't just for show, but a design solution to the impossibility of conventional doors in such a tight, low body. Lamborghini would later adopt the concept for the Countach, cementing it in the mythology of Italian supercars. But it started here. This was ground zero for the wedge era.

Even the Carabo's colour scheme was a deliberate act of provocation. The iridescent green paint, flecked with metallic sheen, was unlike anything else on the road. But it was the windows that truly caught the eye: a shimmering gold tint that gave the glass a mysterious, almost impenetrable aura. Not merely decorative, the golden hue was achieved using vapour-deposited metal oxide film – a cutting-edge aerospace material at the time.

And then there was the flash orange and green. The Carabo's vivid accents, especially around the tail and intake grilles, weren't chosen purely for drama.

Behind the Bertone badge lies the work of its design chief and undisputed master of wedge design – the brilliant Marcello Gandini.

Flashes of neon colour at the car's extremities enhance its visibility: futurism put to work for safety.

They were also functional: meant to make the vehicle more visible on the road or track, a safety cue borrowed from high-visibility gear and racing livery.

Beneath its aluminium body panels, the Carabo was based on Alfa Romeo's Tipo 33 Stradale (chassis #750.33.109.), itself one of the most sophisticated sports cars of the time. Its 2.0-litre V8 engine had been developed for endurance racing: light, compact and screaming to over 10,000 rpm. The chassis was a magnesium-rich tubular structure designed by Autodelta, Alfa's competition division. So despite its show-car persona, the Carabo could run, if needed. But that was never its destiny.

Instead, it became a lightning rod, instantly influencing not only the future of Lamborghini but of the entire Italian design language. Gandini's wedge would be echoed in the Countach, the Lancia Stratos Zero, the Maserati Boomerang and the Ferrari Modulo. Even the angular lines of the Lotus Esprit and the BMW M1 trace back to the Carabo's audacity. It marked a shift from sculpture to statement, from automotive beauty to automotive iconoclasm.

The name came from nature: *Carabus auratus*, the green beetle with iridescent wings. The connection was more than visual. It was symbolic. Nature's most dazzling creations often serve no practical purpose. The Carabo didn't need one either. It was pure provocation. An artefact from the future.

And yet, despite all this, the Carabo remains a singular object. It was never meant for production. Never replicated. Never diluted. Just one was built, and it has remained in the care of Alfa Romeo since its debut in 1968.

Which makes this moment – photographing it under open skies outside the Museo Storico – something quietly miraculous. A lone futuristic spark from the past, standing still just long enough to be captured. Even now, over fifty years later, the Carabo does what it was designed to do: stop the world, and make us look twice. ■

Beneath the futuristic bodywork lies genuine racing machinery: the Carabo, based on the Alfa Romeo 33 Stradale, is powered by the same remarkable 2.0-litre V8.

ALFA ROMEO CARABO

1968
One-off
V8 engine (1,995 cc)
230 hp
260 km/h

1970

LANCIA STRATOS ZERO

STRAIGHT FROM ANOTHER PLANET

LA TÊTE DE CHIEN, FRANCE

GOOD YEAR
GOOD YEAR

Try to imagine the shock this car must have caused in 1970: the Stratos Zero was undoubtedly the most extreme car ever unveiled.

When the Lancia Stratos Zero first appeared in 1970, most people weren't sure what they were seeing. It was as if a spacecraft had landed at the Turin Motor Show by mistake, slicing through convention like a blade from another world. The public didn't crowd around it so much as they circled it, cautiously, as if waiting to see if it would hover or speak.

And in a way, it did speak. It told designers, engineers and dreamers everywhere that the future had just begun.

At just 84 cm tall, with a front end that looked like the edge of a razor and a cockpit you entered through the rising windscreen, it disregarded every established rule of automotive form. The car wasn't built to go fast or win races. It was built to be seen, and to change what could be imagined.

It had no grille, no visible doors, no conventional proportions. The body was a radical brown-orange, richly metallic, catching the sun like polished bronze. It glowed. It didn't reflect the world around it – it redefined it. Designed by Marcello Gandini at Bertone, the Zero was an uncompromising act of imagination that would shift the entire language of car design.

Even parked, it looked like it was still moving. Its cabin was accessed by lifting the whole windscreen. The wheels were hidden deep inside the angular bodywork. Headlights emerged like slits from the front. Rear visibility was barely an afterthought. There was a steering wheel, pedals, gauges, but they felt ornamental in a space that seemed destined more for flight than driving.

Its mechanical core was more modest – the mid-mounted 1.6-litre V4 came from the Lancia Fulvia – but that was beside the point. The Stratos Zero was never really about performance. It was about provocation. It was a rolling sculpture, and its presence created a visible fault line between the past and what was to come.

And its colour wasn't just aesthetic flair. The deep brown-orange finish was chosen for maximum visual impact. It was bold enough to stop crowds, yet sophisticated enough to feel calculated, almost ironic. Like everything about the Zero, it played with the very idea of what a car should be.

The Zero wasn't just ahead of its time – it was outside of it. It directly influenced the wedge era of the 1970s and laid the aesthetic groundwork for the production Lancia Stratos HF. That car, more compact

HF

The only way to board this flying saucer without doors is through the windscreen – the steering column shifts aside to allow entry.

Beneath the rear bonnet hides the modest 1.6-litre V4 engine of the Lancia Fulvia: enough to set this aesthetic marvel in motion and prove that this sculpture of the future is, indeed, also a car.

Sharp, pointed forms dominate the car, culminating in the spectacular pyramidal rear bonnet. This vehicle seems to have arrived from another planet.

With this manifesto, Marcello Gandini and the Turin-based coachbuilcer Bertone positioned themselves as the dominant force in automotive design of the 1970s.

and rally-focused, would go on to become a motorsport icon. But the Zero was never meant to be tamed. It was the concept in its rawest, most unfiltered form.

The Zero didn't just influence cars. It slipped into popular culture, appearing in films like *Moonwalker* with Michael Jackson and becoming a visual shorthand for the future in media and design. More than a car, it was a silhouette, a symbol that was copied, studied and reinterpreted endlessly in video games, comics and architecture. It was what the future looked like before the future caught up.

Retained by Bertone for decades, it was eventually sold and meticulously restored to its full glory. Since then, it has emerged only occasionally – always to awe and applause – earning victories at numerous concours of elegance and reaffirming, time and again, its place as one of the most extraordinary objects ever to wear wheels.

To see it now, resting on the rock promontory of the Tête de Chien high above Monaco, is to feel the same chill of disbelief that must have greeted its debut. We chose this place deliberately: a mineral landscape, stark and surreal, echoing the stone quarries and futuristic wastelands where concept cars were once photographed in the 1970s. The site, no longer accessible by car, was a rare and fleeting stage for this relic of the impossible. There, above the clouds and far from the ordinary, the Stratos Zero looks exactly where it belongs.

And maybe that's the final truth of the Stratos Zero. It doesn't need movement to feel fast, or sound to feel loud. Just being here, on Earth, is provocative enough. ■

Marcello Gandini didn't just design the bodywork – he conceived the interior, the wheels and even the logos of his concept cars: a genius of multifaceted talent.

GOOD YEAR

LANCIA STRATOS ZERO

1970
One-off
V4 engine (1,584 cc)
115 hp
230 km/h

1970

MERCEDES-BENZ C 111-II

A MIRAGE ON ICE

ST. MORITZ, CANTON OF THE GRISONS, SWITZERLAND

Gullwing doors on a Mercedes? The visual nod to its 300 SL ancestor was undoubtedly too tempting to resist, while the vibrant orange colour firmly roots it in its era.

For most, the C 111 is a memory frozen in the pages of magazines – a dream car too bold to live. But here, gliding across the crystalline surface of the frozen St. Moritz lake, it feels real again. Unreal, but real.

While the C 111 began life as a rotary-engine test mule, the second-generation C 111-II – introduced in 1970 and the car you see here – was far more serious, closer to production reality. Built on a lightweight steel spaceframe with fibreglass-reinforced plastic bodywork, it retained the dramatic gullwing doors but featured substantial aerodynamic improvements. The front end was reshaped for better downforce, the rear revised for cooling efficiency, and the wheelbase extended for high-speed stability.

Underneath that otherworldly shape, Mercedes experimented with multiple powerplants. Most famous were the four-rotor Wankel engines producing over 350 horsepower, but two cars were quietly fitted with the M116 3.5-litre V8, borrowed from the 280 SE 3.5 but tuned for mid-engine configuration. These engines offered greater reliability and familiarity, a nod towards real-world viability, and made the car more than just a lab experiment.

The V8-powered C 111-II was capable of zero to 100 km/h in under five seconds, and a top speed of over 270 km/h. Power was delivered through a five-speed ZF manual gearbox, and thanks to its fibreglass body, the car weighed just 1,250 kg.

Suspension was all-independent, with double wishbones up front and a low-mounted multi-link set-up in the rear, derived from Mercedes-Benz's racing knowledge. Four-wheel ventilated disc brakes, large for their time, gave it the stopping power to match its speed.

Inside, the cabin was surprisingly refined for a prototype: form-fitting bucket seats, a comprehensive instrument panel, and forward visibility that defied its dramatic exterior. Even the windows and air conditioning worked properly – this was a concept built with intent.

Only 14 C 111-IIs were constructed, of which just two were V8-powered. Neither was ever publicly offered for sale. Mercedes saw them as testbeds, not showpieces. But even as engineering tools, they captured the public's imagination – an idea of what could have been if Mercedes had taken a different road.

The interior of this concept car is surprisingly close to that of a road car: Mercedes could almost have put it into series production.

The Mercedes C 111 series is best known for its Wankel and diesel engines, but this one, powered by a V8, was the most realistic.

A 1970 prototype on ice? That's the magic of the International Concours of Elegance St. Moritz (The I.C.E.), where the world's most beautiful cars glide across a truly unique stage.

But Mercedes, ever pragmatic, never gave the green light for production. The car was deemed too exotic, too risky. The future it promised would have to wait.

When Mercedes-Benz officially cancelled the C 111 project as a production car, it could have faded quietly into the archives. Instead, it was reborn with a new purpose. No longer chasing the showroom, the C 111 became a precision weapon aimed at the record books. In 1976, a third evolution – known as the C 111-IID – was fitted with a 3.0-litre turbocharged five-cylinder diesel engine, and taken to the Nardò Ring in southern Italy. There, it shattered long-distance speed records, averaging over 252 km/h for 12 hours straight. In 1979, the final iteration, C 111-IV, returned with a twin-turbo V8 and reached 403.978 km/h, briefly making it the fastest car in the world.

What began as an impossible supercar became one of the most effective test platforms ever built, proving the viability of high-performance diesels, turbocharging and advanced aerodynamics. The C 111 never made it to production, but it didn't vanish. It evolved, broke boundaries, and redefined what Mercedes-Benz engineering could do when freed from commercial limits.

And yet, 50 years later, it moves again. On ice. The V8 murmurs beneath that fibreglass shell, now the soundtrack of a ghost in motion. Around it, a crowd hushed by the spectacle, by the surreal collision of eras – futurism from 1970 meeting the eternal snow of the Engadin Alps.

And don't call it orange! The colour is officially known as *Weissherbst* ('white autumn' in German) but in truth, it's a luminous shade of metallic bronze. Chosen to accentuate the C 111's radical curves and sharp edges, it glows like a concept from another world.

It never reached the autobahns. Never fought Ferraris or haunted night-time boulevards. But here, at the International Concours of Elegance St. Moritz (The I.C.E.), it glides like it always belonged. A stillborn supercar, reborn – if only for a moment – on a frozen lake. ■

MERCEDES-BENZ C 111-II

1970
14 prototypes assembled (2 with V8 engine)
V8 engine (3,499 cc)
200 hp
270 km/h

1970

TOYOTA 2000GT

THE SHOGUN'S COUPE

TOKYO, JAPAN

瑞輪寺
全国潮師法縁本部
本山瑞輪寺
横浜402
そ20-00

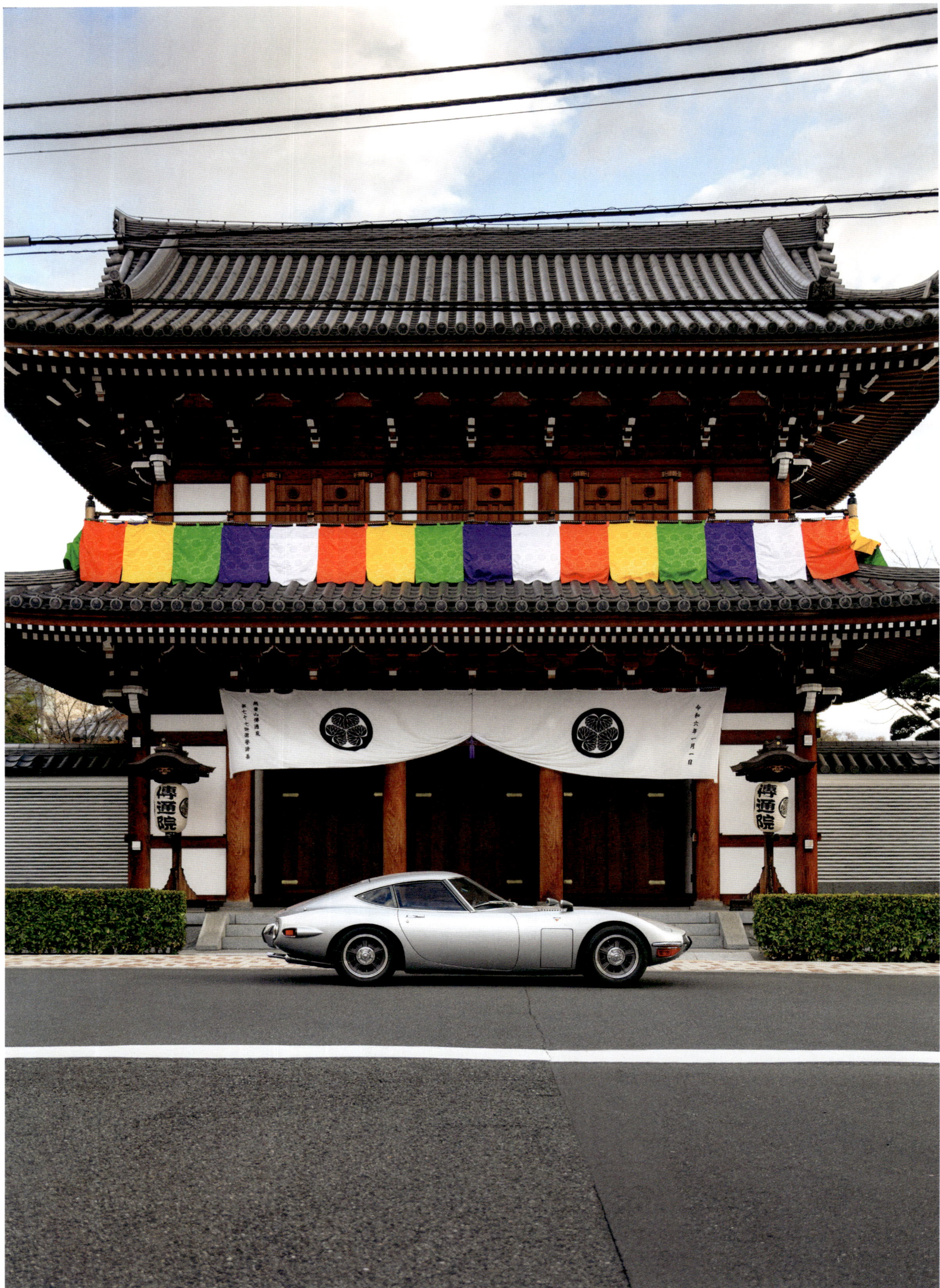
令和六年一月一日
傳通院
傳通院

This elegant coupe is not only Japan's first true high-performance sports car, but also the country's first automobile to become a coveted icon among collectors worldwide – helped, of course, by a certain James Bond.

In the still hush of a Tokyo shrine, where the scent of pine mingles with drifting incense, something glints beneath the torii gates. At first, it could be mistaken for a sacred object: low-slung, impossibly elegant, glimmering in soft silver like a blade drawn under moonlight. But this is no relic. It's a revolution dressed in reverence. A 1970 Toyota 2000GT – Japan's first true sports car, an audacious retort to European dominance, and a quiet prophecy of what the East could become.

By the time this second-series MF10 left Yamaha's factory, the 2000GT was already spoken of in the same breath as Ferraris and Aston Martins. It wasn't just the design – though that, in itself, was radical – nor merely the performance that rivalled Porsche and Jaguar. It was the intent: a car built not just to compete, but to redefine what a Japanese automobile could be.

The project began as a collaboration between Toyota and Yamaha in the early '60s. Yamaha, then better known for pianos and motorcycles, had previously worked with Nissan on a shelved sports car. Toyota picked up the pieces, saw the potential, and handed Yamaha a solid but unremarkable inline-six from the Crown. What came back was a transformed 2.0-litre DOHC masterpiece: 150 horsepower, three twin-barrel Mikuni-Solex carburettors, and a sound that blended straight-six silk with racing urgency.

That engine, paired with a five-speed manual gearbox, sat low and far back in a custom chassis with near-perfect 51:49 weight distribution. The body – a collaboration with designer Satoru Nozaki – was a sculpture of aluminium curves. Just 45 inches tall, with pop-up headlights, flush door handles, a tapering nose and fastback tail, the car had the presence of a mid-engine exotic. It didn't look like it was inspired by the Jaguar E-Type – it looked ready to outgrow it.

Inside, it was even more remarkable. The rosewood trim wasn't just decorative: it was handcrafted by Yamaha's piano division, the same artisans who built concert grands. Paired with magnesium-alloy fixtures and a cockpit designed for tactility and clarity, the cabin had the soul of a symphony hall. Driving it wasn't just athletic – it was sensorial.

Only 351 units were built from 1967 to 1970. Of those, fewer than 100 were second-series MF10s like this one, with subtle improvements to mechanical reliability and trim. This particular car, chassis #MF10-10460, was finished in light silver metallic and has remained in the same Tokyo district since new.

Its legacy defies its production numbers. The 2000GT wasn't merely Japan's first great sports car –

Smaller glass-covered headlights define the front of the second-series 2000GT, giving it a more mature and elegant presence.

A hidden masterpiece: the car's fine woodwork was entrusted to Yamaha's craftsmen, specialists in piano-making.

it was Japan's first collectable one. It set international speed and endurance records, appeared in *You Only Live Twice* as a one-off convertible for Sean Connery, beat Porsche and Alfa Romeo at Fuji, raced at Sebring, and was campaigned in the US under Carroll Shelby. It did all of this with grace and humility, a katana among sabres.

Unlike its brash Western peers, the 2000GT never shouted. It was elegant, measured and precise. And yet, it didn't last. At over $7,000 in the US, it was more expensive than a Jaguar E-Type or Porsche 911. It wasn't profitable, but it was unforgettable.

Today, the 2000GT is spoken of with reverence. It became the first Japanese classic to cross the million-dollar threshold at auction, confirming its status not just in Japan, but on the global stage. It remains the most desirable Japanese car ever built – a founding myth on wheels. Toyota wouldn't build another car of such purity until the Lexus LFA, nearly forty years later, and even that modern marvel still lived in the 2000GT's shadow.

This very car lives a quiet but active life. Living in Nerima district since 1970, it is now owned by an American who spends part of the year in Japan – and drives it. Regularly. From Tokyo to his retreat in Atami, Shizuoka, it's not a garage queen but a moving monument.

And perhaps that's why, under the shrine's eaves and among the whispering trees, it looks so completely at peace. Not just a car, but a tribute – to craftsmanship, to ambition, to a nation that chose to lead by design rather than imitation. And in doing so, gave the world a masterpiece. ■

A modest 2.0-litre six-cylinder at its core, the engine was transformed by Yamaha with an aluminium dual-overhead-cam cylinder head featuring hemispherical chambers and three dual-throat Mikuni carburettors.

横浜402
そ 20-00

TOYOTA 2000GT

1967–1970
351 units produced
Straight-six engine (1,998 cc)
150 hp
220 km/h

1973

PORSCHE 911 CARRERA RS 2.7

LA VIE EN ROSE

PONT NEUF, PARIS, FRANCE

Carrera

Only four 911 Carrera RS 2.7 models were ever painted in this vibrant *Fraise* – strawberry – hue, made even more radiant by the golden-hour sunlight.

Few cars carry a legacy as foundational as the 911 Carrera RS 2.7. Introduced in 1972 for the 1973 model year, it was Porsche's answer to new Group 4 racing homologation rules, which required a minimum of 500 road cars to be produced. Porsche expected to struggle to sell them. They sold all 500 in a matter of weeks. Then another 500. Then another 580. A legend was born almost by accident.

The RS 2.7 was the first production Porsche 911 to wear the Carrera name – a nod to the company's victories in the Carrera Panamericana – and the first road-going 911 to be developed directly from racing experience. It combined a larger, more powerful engine with a lighter shell and upgraded aerodynamics, turning the friendly 911 into a focused performance machine.

At its heart was a 2,687 cc flat-six engine producing 210 horsepower at 6,300 rpm and 255 Nm of torque. That power, paired with a kerb weight of just over 1,000 kg in Sport (M471) trim – or around 1,075 kg for Touring (M472) models like this one – gave the car remarkable pace for its day: zero to 100 km/h in 5.8 seconds, and a top speed of 240 km/h. Just as important was the feel: sharpened suspension geometry, Bilstein dampers, reinforced rear trailing arms and revised weight distribution made the RS 2.7 a joy to drive fast.

But its most visible innovation was the *Entenbürzel* – the ducktail. This was Porsche's first road car to wear a rear spoiler, developed after extensive wind tunnel testing at Stuttgart. Modest in size but radical in impact, the ducktail reduced rear-end lift by up to 75% at speed, dramatically improving stability. It also helped define the 911's shape for decades. The RS 2.7 wasn't just faster – it was smarter.

This car – chassis #9113600171 – is a Touring model, meaning it retains the comforts of the standard 911S: full carpeting, sound insulation, reclining seats and a more refined interior. But it's anything but ordinary. Painted *Fraise* (Strawberry), code LO2491, it is one of only four RS 2.7s delivered in this striking pink hue. Unmistakable, it turns the RS's aggressive arches and purposeful lines into something unexpectedly elegant and completely unforgettable.

Delivered new to Germany just days before Christmas in 1972, chassis #9113600171 arrived at the Raffay Volkswagen-Porsche dealership in Hamburg. Its first caretaker? Günther Wilfried Noll, an engine builder and tuner with a reputation as spirited as the cars he prepared. The RS left the factory fitted with a few carefully chosen options: black leatherette Recaro sport seats with Perlon fabric inserts, headrests included. Purpose met taste.

But its early life was anything but restrained. In April 1981, Noll entered the car in the infamous Cannonball Europe, an open-road endurance run not so much sanctioned as survived. Period photographs show the car in a wild configuration: honeycomb wheels, apple-green script across its underbody, and the stance of a car driven in anger. So notorious was his high-speed behaviour that, for the 1982 Cannonball, Noll returned

Carrera

Porsche's racing heritage is evident in the central tachometer and in the 2.7-litre flat-six engine with mechanical fuel injection, its cylinders treated with Nikasil for maximum performance.

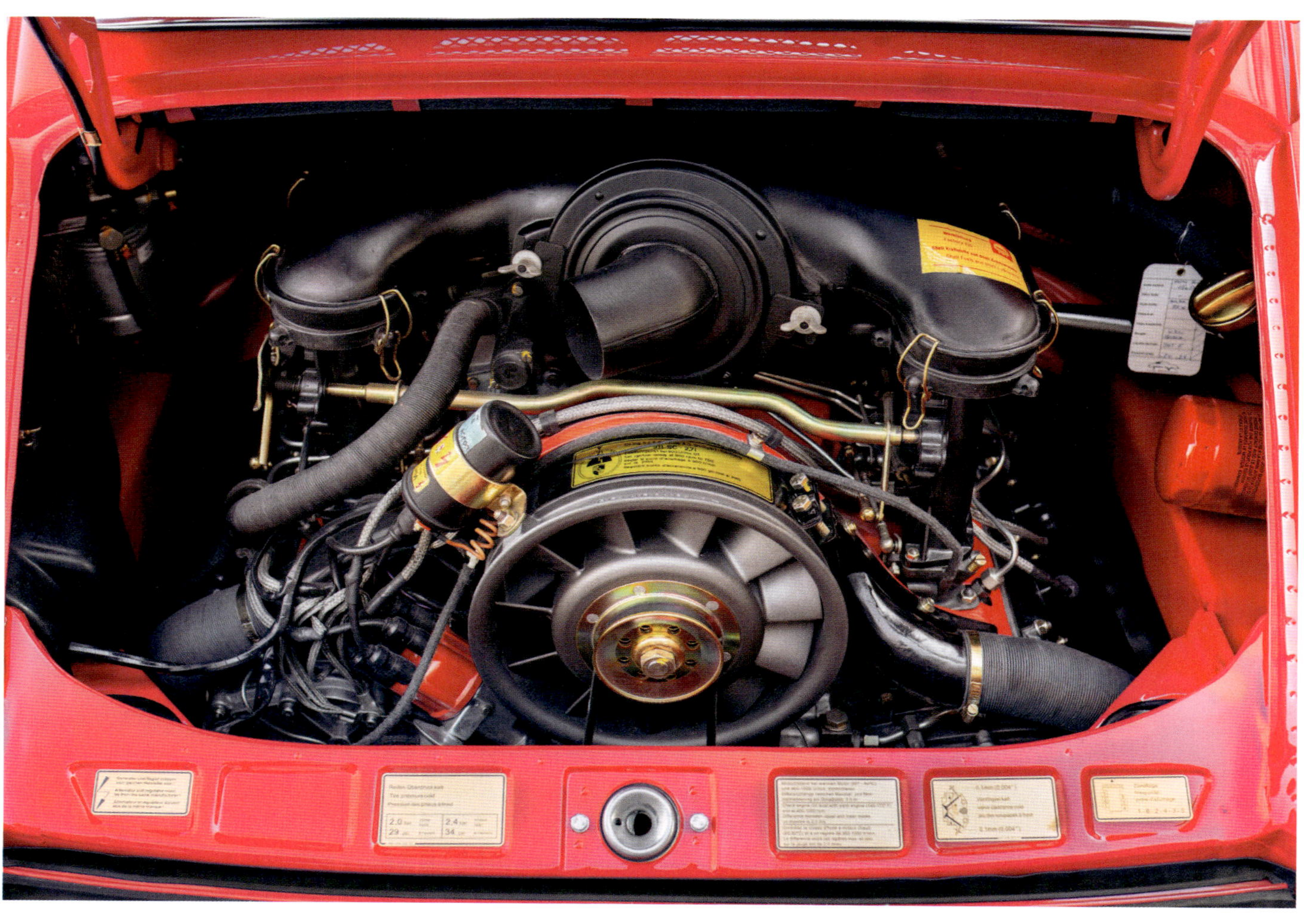

The icon: the very first spoiler fitted to a Porsche road car, it improved both aerodynamic downforce and engine cooling. Most importantly, it reduced drag, boosting top speed.

This car comes equipped with the Touring package, like most Carrera RS 2.7 models: less stripped-down than the Sport version, it remained a true road car while delivering competition-level performance.

with the car repainted in Gulf livery and fitted with orange wheels – a disguise to outpace not just rivals, but the law. He also swapped in a 3.0 RS engine, upping the stakes even further.

Over time, that engine gave way to a 2.8, and the original unit – like so many stories from the era – was lost, likely stolen. The car changed hands. Then, at some point, it returned to its factory *Fraise* pink. In 1987, it was acquired by Udo Kruse, a seasoned driver who brought the car back to fighting form. In his hands, it became a familiar sight on the podium at Zandvoort, Hockenheim and the Nürburgring in historic racing throughout the early 2000s.

Now, lovingly restored and living in France, this RS wears its history with pride. Photographed at dawn on the Pont Neuf in Paris, it looks perfectly at ease. The oldest bridge in the city paired with a car that became the bridge between Porsche's racing dominance and its road-going mythology. This RS has been restored with meticulous care. Every surface, every seam, feels ready to race – or just to disappear down a winding mountain pass.

The Carrera RS 2.7 marked the beginning of Porsche's modern performance lineage: it directly inspired the 3.0 RS, the 934, the 964 RS and every GT3 that followed. More than a collector's item, it's the cornerstone of Porsche's identity.

And this one, in *Fraise*, is its most playful expression, the unicorn among unicorns. You don't just see it. You remember it. ■

PORSCHE 911 CARRERA RS 2.7

1972–1973
1,590 units produced
Flat-six engine (2,687 cc)
210 hp
240 km/h

1977

LAMBORGHINI COUNTACH LP400 'PERISCOPIO'

THE MOST ECCENTRIC UFO OF SANT'AGATA

DUBAI DESERT, UNITED ARAB EMIRATES

77 UFO

countach
77
UFO

Another pair of iconic doors: the famous 'lambo-doors' or scissor doors, derived from the ones Marcello Gandini had already designed for the Alfa Romeo Carabo. The Countach is its true spiritual heir.

There are moments in design when a line is drawn and everything changes. The Lamborghini Countach did just that with a ruler and a razor blade. In 1971, it crashed onto the stage like a spacecraft from an Italian fever dream. And by the time production began in 1974, the world had still not caught up. This was not a car. It was a statement. A threat. A glimpse of something radically new.

The example pictured here – chassis #1120248 – is a 1977 LP400, and it wears its identity like a badge of honour: *77 UFO*. It's the kind of detail you couldn't invent, nor would you need to. The plate says it all. Built in 1977, and looking like it dropped from orbit. No name could better capture the way this machine crashed into the automotive consciousness: alien, angular and utterly other.

Painted in a rare *Viola* metallic and trimmed in white leather, the car strikes a dramatic contrast even here in the endless light and warm stillness of the Dubai desert. It's what aficionados call a *Periscopio*, named after the recessed roof channel and mirror set-up meant to improve rearward visibility. It's a rare detail, abandoned in later versions, and one of many clues that this is no ordinary Countach.

The LP400 was the Countach in its purest, most undiluted form. Only 157 were made, each shaped and assembled largely by hand at Bertone. Marcello Gandini's design was radical even by his standards: a wedge of matte aggression with scissor doors, shark-gill intakes and impossibly low lines, just 106.5 cm tall. The absence of spoilers, flares or wings makes it feel even more futuristic. Later Countachs may have been louder, but none were more precise.

Beneath its engine cover sits a longitudinal 3.9-litre V12, fed by six Weber carburettors and producing around 375 horsepower. The gearbox is mounted ahead of the engine, with a driveshaft running beneath it – a unique layout that kept the car compact and balanced. Performance figures were outrageous for the day: zero to 100 km/h in under six seconds, and a top speed close to 300 km/h. But it was the *way* it delivered that speed – raw, metallic and unfiltered – that left an impression.

There's a clarity to this version that later models lost. No bloat. No theatrical wings or swollen arches. Just pure intent on magnesium Campagnolo wheels. It's still a wild car – difficult, loud and physical – but also honest. It talks to the driver, and demands a response.

1977. Its first owner was Michael D. Noss, an entrepreneur and gentleman racer with a flair for the dramatic. Noss didn't just want any Countach; he wanted *his* Countach. Finished in *Viola Metallizzato* over a white

The 'Periscopio' is the Countach in its purest form, yet the engineers had to add air intakes on the fenders and doors to cool the engine, which Gandini was absolutely furious about.

The licence plate is telling: few cars have ever been more futuristic than the Countach. Even today, it remains a UFO on the road.

The groove carved into the roof is the remnant of a periscope-style rear-view system, abandoned before production – a distinctive feature of the very first Countach.

leather interior, it arrived as one of the most flamboyant LP400s ever configured. Noss reportedly wouldn't let anyone else drive it – not even his wife – and outfitted it with features that bordered on the surreal: a white telephone mounted atop the dashboard, white-painted accents outlining every panel and intake, white wheel rims, and even a single white handprint on the rear right wing – an eccentric signature left unexplained.

It was a UFO among UFOs. Unsurprisingly, this bold expression didn't please every subsequent custodian. At some point in its history, the car was stripped of its theatrical character, repainted in yellow and retrimmed with a brown interior as a more conservative disguise for a car that was never meant to blend in.

It wasn't until 2016 that the Countach was given a new lease of life. Entrusted to the renowned Modena-based specialists Bacchelli & Villa, the car underwent a meticulous restoration. During the process, the unmistakable flash of metallic purple beneath layers of yellow paint told its own story. Bit by bit, the car's original identity resurfaced. The *Viola* hue was matched, the factory details reinstated.

Today, it appears exactly as it did in 1977 – minus the phone, handprint and personal touches of its Swedish original owner. What remains is a Countach LP400 restored to full factory specification, but with a story richer than most.

And then there's the plate. *77 UFO*. It's more than clever. It's a timestamp. A declaration. A fitting marker for a machine that looked like it belonged to another era – or another planet. The world has changed a lot since 1977, but the LP400 still looks like tomorrow.

In the rising sun over the desert, sand whispering at its wheels, it doesn't feel like it's looking back. It never did. ■

You'd be surprised at how small the Countach really is, and later cars featured a raised roof. Yet, somehow, Lamborghini still managed to squeeze in the magnificent 3.9-litre V12.

77 UFO

LAMBORGHINI COUNTACH LP400 'PERISCOPIO'

1974–1978
157 units produced
V12 engine (3,929 cc)
370 hp
300 km/h

LANCIA RALLY 037 'STRADALE'

STAGE READY

CANTON OF VAUD, SWITZERLAND

VD · 19874

If you squint, you might catch faint hints that the car is loosely based on a Lancia Beta Montecarlo – but in truth, it's the homologation version of a true Group B racer. Note the double roof bulge, designed to free up space for the drivers' helmets.

The narrow vineyard roads of Switzerland's Vaud canton wind and dip like the ribboned trails of a rally stage. Morning mist hangs low over the vines, and the damp tarmac is etched with hairpins that seem made for momentum. And then, there's the sound. Mechanical, raw, spooling with a sting – and around the bend comes the unmistakable silhouette of the Lancia 037 Stradale, painted in rally red and rumbling as if Group B never ended.

Homologation was never supposed to be this beautiful. The 037 was born in a moment of rebellion and revival. At the dawn of the 1980s, Lancia – battered by the winds of Fiat's corporate consolidation – found itself facing the future of rallying. The Fulvia and Stratos were legends past. The all-wheel-drive Audi Quattro was rewriting the rules. But in the corridors of Abarth and Lancia Corse, there was still belief in simplicity: lightness, balance and a driver's right foot. And so, the 037 was forged, an analogue warrior in a digital war.

Its DNA was a hybrid of innovation and necessity. Built on the basic platform of the Lancia Beta Montecarlo, the 037 shared little more than a conceptual outline with its sibling. The central tub was derived from the Beta, but radically reworked with Kevlar and fibreglass body panels. A tubular rear subframe was added to accommodate a new suspension layout and drivetrain geometry. Gone was the mid-mounted transverse engine of the Montecarlo; in its place sat a longitudinally mounted, 2.0-litre inline-four developed by Abarth, dry-sumped and supercharged by a large volumetric compressor.

In road-going Stradale form, that engine produced around 205 horsepower – not an outrageous figure, but in a car weighing just 1,170 kg, it was more than enough. The torque curve was punchy and immediate, thanks to the mechanical Roots-type supercharger, and power delivery was linear – a far cry from the turbocharged monsters that would follow. The five-speed manual gearbox was perfectly matched to the engine's character, and the 037's steering, unassisted and pure, made even modest roads feel like rally stages.

But behind the performance was intent. Lancia needed to build 200 road cars to homologate the 037 for Group B rally competition. Each Stradale was assembled at Pininfarina and finished with minimal concessions to comfort: sliding windows, thin carpeting, body-hugging seats and little else. It was not luxurious, nor was it trying to be. The red car photographed here,

Inside the tubular frame, the Fiat engine reworked by Abarth and fitted with a supercharger is mounted longitudinally to make life easier for the mechanics.

carving through the vineyard lanes like a stage weapon off duty, carries that same uncompromising DNA.

It looks like a car trying to stay civil, but always ready to snap into combat.

And in combat, it did more than survive – it triumphed. The Lancia 037 holds the distinction of being the last rear-wheel-drive car to win the World Rally Championship. In 1983, against the rising tide of Audi's revolutionary Quattro, Lancia did the impossible: it clinched the Constructors' title. The win was not just mechanical but philosophical – a celebration of purity, agility and tireless engineering. It won rallies in Corsica, New Zealand, Greece and Sanremo, thanks to legends like Walter Röhrl, Markku Alén and Attilio Bettega, whose feedback helped refine the car into a scalpel-sharp tool.

Though it would eventually be eclipsed by the all-wheel-drive Delta S4, the 037's legacy is one of defiance and elegance. It was a car built on the edge of obsolescence but driven with the heart of champions.

Visually, it remains one of the most purposeful designs of its era. The shape – compact, taut, slightly aggressive – was a blend of function and flair. The nose was low and flat, with inset round headlights and a scooped hood for cooling. The rear haunches flared around staggered-width wheels, and the engine bay was topped by a black mesh panel that seemed almost too race-ready for the road. In Stradale form, it wore no liveries, just body-coloured form and presence. But every vent, scoop and flare served a purpose.

Here, photographed on this winding Swiss vineyard road, the 037 is far from the dust and gravel of the Acropolis or Corsica. And yet, it looks perfectly at home – perched between elegance and aggression, between wine country serenity and rally-stage savagery. The Lancia 037 wasn't just the end of an era. It was its last great firework. ■

Fuses accessible right on the dashboard, exposed reinforcement bars, bucket seats – no doubt about it, this is a true rally car.

The massive rear spoiler from the racing versions was fitted to only a few 037 Stradales – rally drivers used to say it slowed the car down like a parachute!

LANCIA RALLY 037 'STRADALE'

1982–1983
262 units produced
Straight-four engine (1,995 cc)
205 hp
220 km/h

1985

FERRARI 288 GTO

THE LAST CLASSIC

HERTFORDSHIRE, GREAT BRITAIN

The 288 GTO looks like a 308 GTB, but is wider to accommodate larger wheels, and above all longer to allow for a longitudinal mounting of the V8 engine.

Tucked between brick barns, the black Ferrari barely stirs the still air. There's no crowd here. No flashing lights or velvet ropes. Just the hush of a farm court in the English countryside – a stage far from the world of Brunei royalty, from Maranello's gates or from the Paris salons where Ferraris were once unveiled like sculptures. And yet, it fits. A final curtain call often deserves a quiet exit.

This is not just any 288 GTO. It is one of the rarest: a factory right-hand-drive car, delivered new in 1985 and once owned by Prince Jefri Bolkiah, brother to the Sultan of Brunei and one of the most enigmatic and lavish car collectors in modern history. His collection, at its zenith, is said to have surpassed 3,000 vehicles. Mercedes and Porsches. Bentleys by the dozen. Ferrari specials no one else could order. Coachbuilt one-offs. And, among them, this: a black GTO, almost sinister in its restraint.

Ferrari wasn't planning on creating a legend when it developed the 288 GTO (officially just called Ferrari GTO). Its birth was practical – a homologation requirement for Group B racing. But as the project evolved, and the race category went up in flames and regulation, the GTO escaped the fate of so many competition cars. It never raced.

The 288 GTO represented a bridge between two eras. Underneath its Pininfarina-designed skin – more aggressive than a 308, yet deceptively similar – lay a tubular steel spaceframe and Kevlar panels. Its twin-turbocharged 2.8-litre V8 sat longitudinally, not transversely, delivering 400 horsepower through a five-speed manual. It was lightweight, brutal and sharp-edged. Zero to 100 km/h in under five seconds. A top speed of 305 km/h. In 1984, that was stratospheric.

The rear was cut high, with massive flared arches and black slats that screamed purpose. The ride was firm. The steering, heavy. There was nothing ornamental about the GTO. It was, in many ways, the last Ferrari engineered without compromise. No electronic aids. No power steering. No softness. Just boost, grip and noise.

The GTO never turned a wheel in competition, but it lit the fuse. Without it, there would be no F40. No F50. No Enzo. It created the template – the bloodline – of Ferrari's modern supercar. But it did so with the restraint of another time. Compared to the winged, exaggerated Ferraris of the '90s and 2000s, the GTO feels almost quiet. Taut. Measured. Classic.

And in this particular example, that balance is amplified. The black paint removes the theatricality, leaving only the form: the pressed fenders, the tucked cabin, the impossibly wide rear track. Inside, the car is sparse – leather bucket seats, Veglia gauges, gated shifter. Nothing superfluous. A car for a prince, but not a toy. A weapon.

It is said that the Brunei royal family's car collection was amassed in secrecy, stored in temperature-controlled warehouses, hidden from the world. Many of

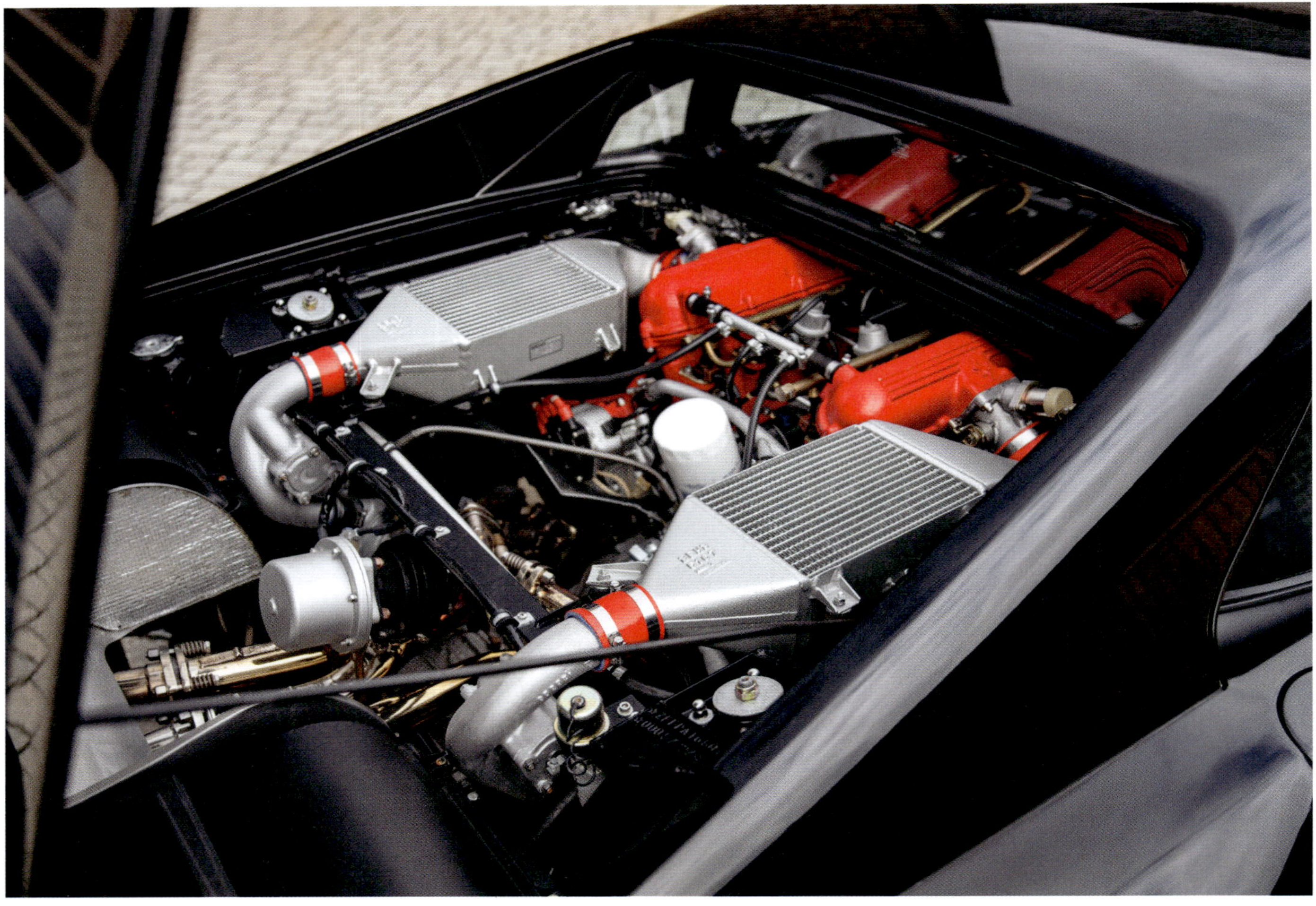

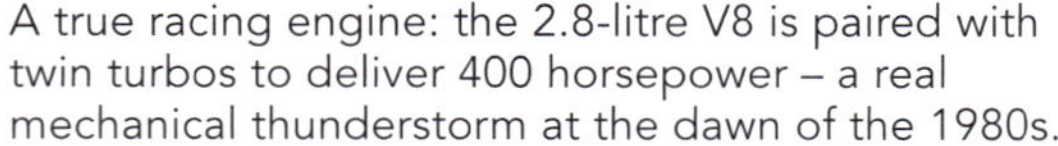

A true racing engine: the 2.8-litre V8 is paired with twin turbos to deliver 400 horsepower – a real mechanical thunderstorm at the dawn of the 1980s.

All GTOs left the Maranello factory painted in red with left-hand drive, but this one had a very special owner: Prince Jefri of Brunei.

The modifications to the car were carried out afterwards by Pininfarina's special projects team – as with many of Prince Jefri's other cars.

Officially, the car is simply called 'GTO'; the '288' is an informal designation used to distinguish it from the 250 GTO.

the cars were never seen. Some were lost. Others, like this GTO, eventually emerged, carrying with them the weight of myth. This car didn't vanish and today stands as one of the finest surviving examples.

Curiously, none of Prince Jefri's four Ferrari 288 GTOs were acquired new. Each was a carefully selected used example, later reimagined to his exacting tastes. Chassis #55671 – the 150th GTO built – was no exception. Originally finished in *Rosso Corsa* and configured in left-hand drive, as any GTO, it left the Ferrari factory in Maranello on 24 April 1985, collected by British Ferrari dealer Ron Stratton for his personal use. After changing hands several times, it was exported to Hong Kong in 1990, before quietly joining the Brunei royal fleet in 1993.

From there, it was sent to Pininfarina, where Paolo Garella's special projects team transformed it into something even more singular. Like the other three GTOs commissioned by the prince, it was finished in a bespoke colour scheme – this one in *Dark Slate* with a red accent stripe – and re-trimmed with a full leather interior. Each of the four bore a unique colour, a private code within a collection that was anything but ordinary.

There's something poetic about ending the book here, in the quiet presence of a black 288 GTO. Because this was the final one. The last car before digital dashboards. Before traction control and carbon tubs. The last Ferrari where the legend still outweighed the technology. The final chapter of the analogue age.

And just as this story closes, another begins. The Porsche 959 – its technological antithesis – would fill the first chapter of another book. One about the digital, the futuristic, the surgically precise. But that's another story. This one ends with a heartbeat, not a binary code. ■

FERRARI 288 GTO

1984–1987
272 units produced
V8 engine (2,855 cc)
400 hp
305 km/h

ACKNOWLEDGEMENTS

I never imagined I'd be here today, working among brilliant and passionate people and photographing the rarest and most beautiful classic cars on Earth. It has been a long journey, but I hope it is only the beginning.

Behind every image lies a strong network of support and inspiration, without which this project would not have been possible. I extend my gratitude to Carolijn Domensino, Eline Maeyens and the team from Lannoo for believing in me and including my vision without any question. Once again, thanks to my friend Yan-Alexandre Damasiewicz for writing my second book with all these fantastic texts and stories. We all learnt a lot thanks to your words and pen. Merci Oliver Camelin, Managing Director EMEA from Gooding Christie's, for your great help.

A huge thank you to all the private collectors and organisations who entrusted me with their iconic cars. Thank you for allowing me the privilege of capturing their beauty and essence in stunning locations. Your generosity has enriched this book immeasurably: Clive Beecham; Jerzy Reczeck; Josef Rettenmaier; Ferdi & Wolfgang Porsche; Filip Baert; Daniel Iseli / Iseli Collection; William Loughran; Chris Wilson; Gregor Fisken / Fiskens; Olivier & Antoine Cazalières; Fritz Burkard / The Pearl Collection; Albert Spiess; Ja Kuba Pietrzak / La Squadra; Museo Alfa Romeo; Mercedes-Benz Museum; Eric Meltzer; Phillip Sarofim; Simon Kidston / Kidston Motor Cars; Jacques Ganem; Jeremy Rollet / Drive Vintage; James Cottingham / DK Engineering.

Behind the scenes, there is a team of unsung heroes whose contributions have been indispensable. Your efforts have played a vital role in bringing this vision to life: Matthieu Lamoure / Artcurial Motorcars; Pierre Novikoff; Anne-Claire Mandine; Maciéj Salasiński / DACAR classics & sports; Pedro Cappelle / Classiche Masters / Alfieri Magazine; Jasper De Smet / KB Technics; Elisabeth Murkovic; Zoltan Szaveri; Hannes Müller; HK-Engineering; Aimery Dutheil; Emanuele Collo; Guido Scassellati Sforzolini; Mathieu Debarges; Kidston Motorcars; Armin Planert; Dana Grote; Romain Bois / Heritage Motors Cars; La Squadra; Lorenzo Ardizio; Raffaella Quaquaro; Museo Alfa Romeo; Mercedes-Benz Museum; The I.C.E. St. Moritz; Classic Driver; Błażej Żuławski; Clark Sopper; Ken Masaito; Scott McIntosh; Geoffroy Peter; David Hervé / RV Classic.

From the bottom of my heart, I want to thank my incredible wife Sophie. The year 2025 has indeed been special, as we got married in May of this year. I also want to thank my best friend Arthur for the countless calls and the laughs, and my parents Eric and Fabienne, the kindest people I know on this planet, who have supported me in every step of my life.

Finally, I extend my heartfelt appreciation to the readers who embark on this visual journey with me. May these images ignite your imagination, evoke emotions, and stir your passion for classic automobiles still further.

Kevin Van Campenhout, 2025

Photography Kevin Van Campenhout
Text Yan-Alexandre Damasiewicz
Editing Heather Sills
Book design Han van de Ven

Sign up for our newsletter with news about new and forthcoming publications on art, interior design, food & travel, photography and fashion as well as exclusive offers and events. If you have any questions or comments about the material in this book, please do not hesitate to contact our editorial team: art@lannoo.com

THEMA: WGCB, AJCD
D/2025/45/560
ISBN: 978-90-209-3062-7
www.lannoo.com